Scale 1: 500,000
or 8 miles to 1 inch
(5km to 1cm)

Reprinted July 2016
15th edition August 2015

© AA Media Limited 2016

Cartography:
All cartography in this atlas edited, designed and produced by the Mapping Services Department of AA Publishing (A05488).

This atlas contains Ordnance Survey data © Crown copyright and database right 2016.

 This is based upon Crown Copyright and is reproduced with the permission of Land & Property Services under delegated authority from the Controller of Her Majesty's Stationery Office, © Crown copyright and database right 2016. PMLPA No. 100497.

 © Ordnance Survey Ireland/ Government of Ireland. Copyright Permit No. MP000616.

Publisher's notes:
Published by AA Publishing (a trading name of AA Media Limited, whose registered office is Fanum House, Basing View, Basingstoke, Hampshire RG21 4EA, UK. Registered number 06112600).

ISBN: 978 0 7495 7734 6 (paperback)

ISBN: 978 0 7495 7733 9 (wire bound)

A CIP Catalogue record for this book is available from the British Library.

Disclaimer:
The contents of this atlas are believed to be correct at the time of the latest revision, it will not contain any subsequent amended, new or temporary information including diversions and traffic control or enforcement systems. The publishers cannot be held responsible or liable for any loss or damage occasioned to any person acting or refraining from action as a result of any use or reliance on material in this atlas, nor for any errors, omissions or changes in such material. This does not affect your statutory rights.

The publishers would welcome information to correct any errors or omissions and to keep this atlas up to date. Please write to the Atlas Editor, AA Publishing, The Automobile Association, Fanum House, Basing View, Basingstoke, Hampshire RG21 4EA, UK.
E-mail: *roadatlasfeedback@theaa.com*

Printer:
Printed in Italy by G. Canale & C. S.p.A.

Atlas contents

Map pages	II
Road map symbols	1
Road atlas Britain 1:500,000 scale	2–65
Index to places in Britain	66–80
County, administrative area map	66–67
Distance charts	**81 & 90**
Britain	81
Ireland	90
Road atlas Ireland 1:1 million scale	82–89
Index to places in Ireland	91–94
County, administrative area map	91

Map pages

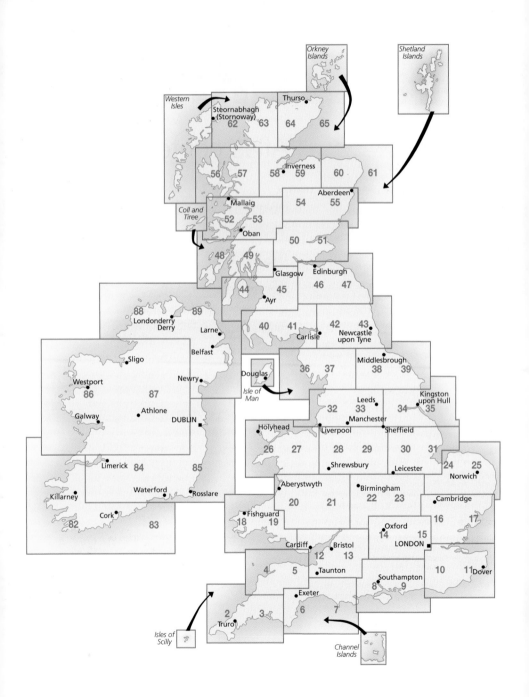

Road map symbols

Britain

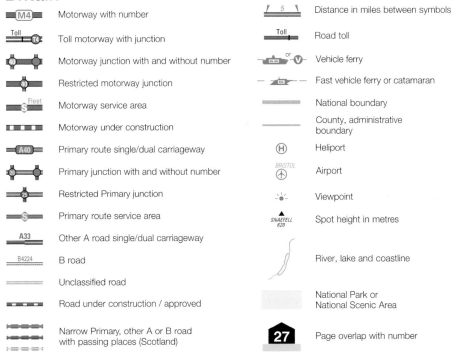

M4	Motorway with number
Toll T4	Toll motorway with junction
40	Motorway junction with and without number
40	Restricted motorway junction
Fleet S	Motorway service area
	Motorway under construction
A40	Primary route single/dual carriageway
25	Primary junction with and without number
25	Restricted Primary junction
S	Primary route service area
A33	Other A road single/dual carriageway
B4224	B road
	Unclassified road
	Road under construction / approved
	Narrow Primary, other A or B road with passing places (Scotland)

5	Distance in miles between symbols
Toll	Road toll
or V	Vehicle ferry
	Fast vehicle ferry or catamaran
	National boundary
	County, administrative boundary
H	Heliport
BRISTOL	Airport
	Viewpoint
SNAEFELL 620	Spot height in metres
	River, lake and coastline
	National Park or National Scenic Area
27	Page overlap with number

1: 500 000

0 — 5 — 10 miles
0 — 5 — 10 — 15 kilometres

8 miles to 1 inch

Ireland

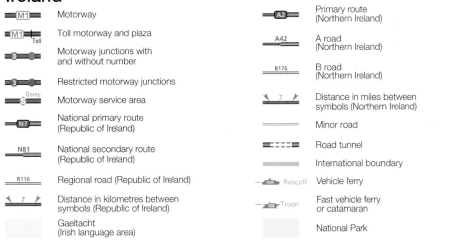

M1	Motorway
M1 Toll	Toll motorway and plaza
3	Motorway junctions with and without number
3	Restricted motorway junctions
Gorey S	Motorway service area
N7	National primary route (Republic of Ireland)
N81	National secondary route (Republic of Ireland)
R116	Regional road (Republic of Ireland)
7	Distance in kilometres between symbols (Republic of Ireland)
	Gaeltacht (Irish language area)

A2	Primary route (Northern Ireland)
A42	A road (Northern Ireland)
B176	B road (Northern Ireland)
7	Distance in miles between symbols (Northern Ireland)
	Minor road
	Road tunnel
	International boundary
Roscoff	Vehicle ferry
Troon	Fast vehicle ferry or catamaran
	National Park

1: 1 000 000

0 — 10 — 20 miles
0 — 10 — 20 — 30 kilometres

16 miles to 1 inch

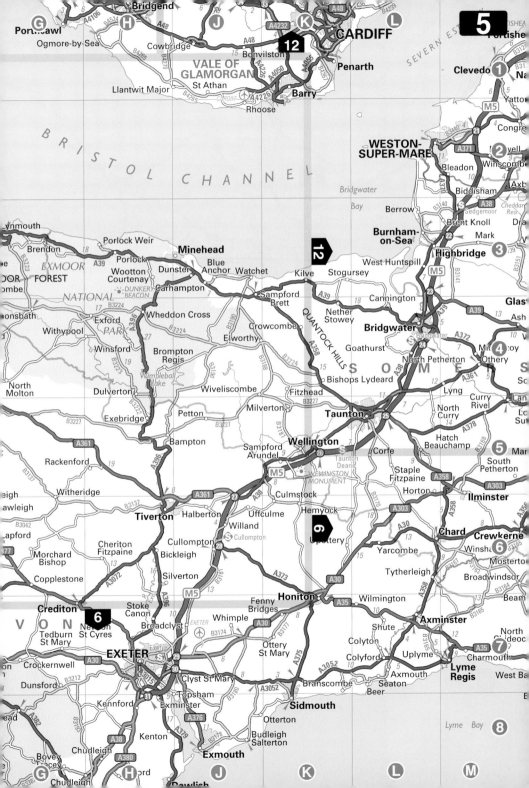

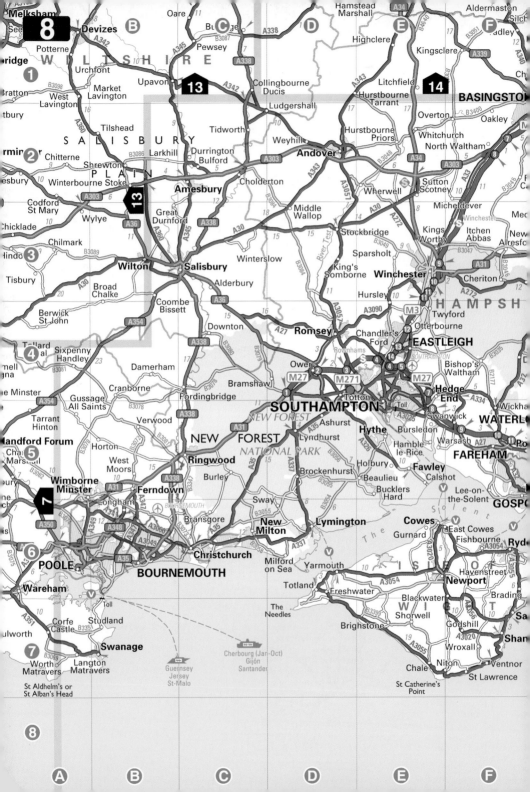

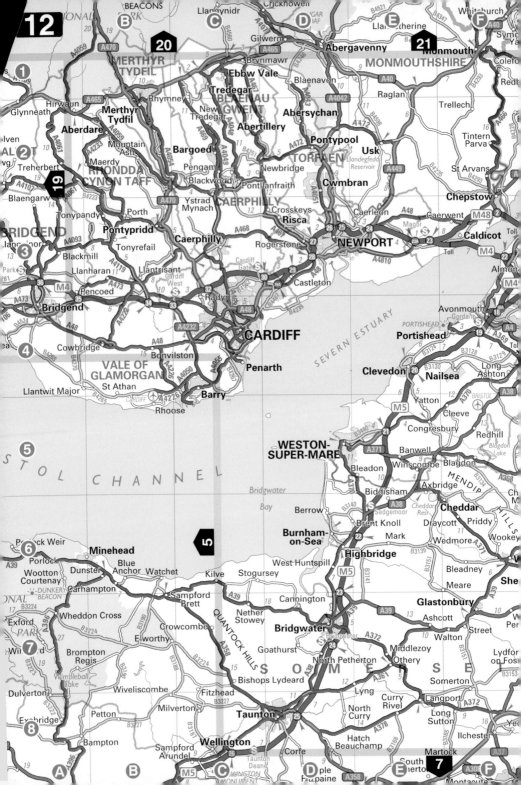

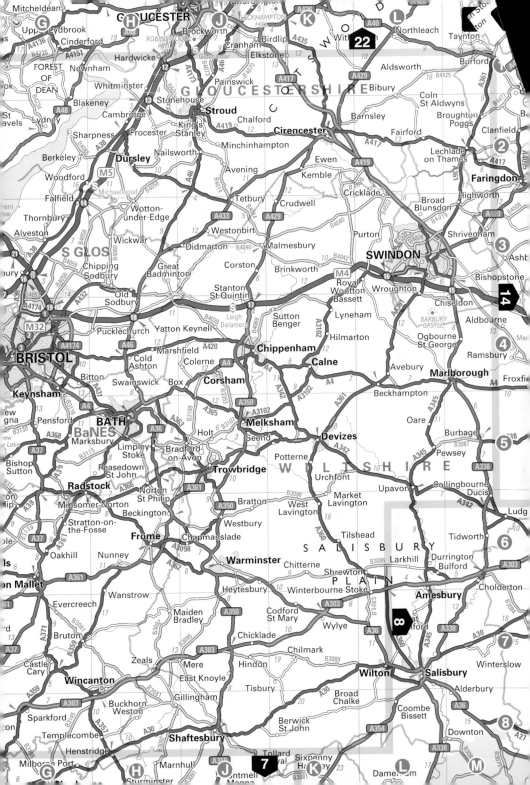

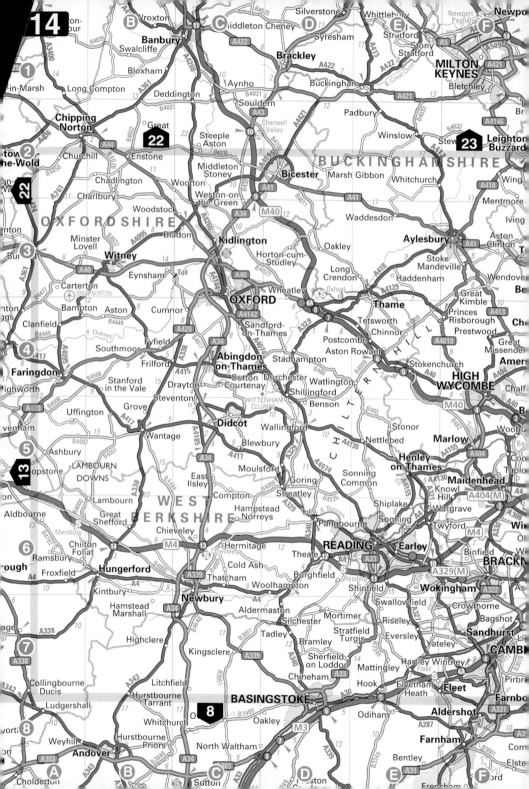

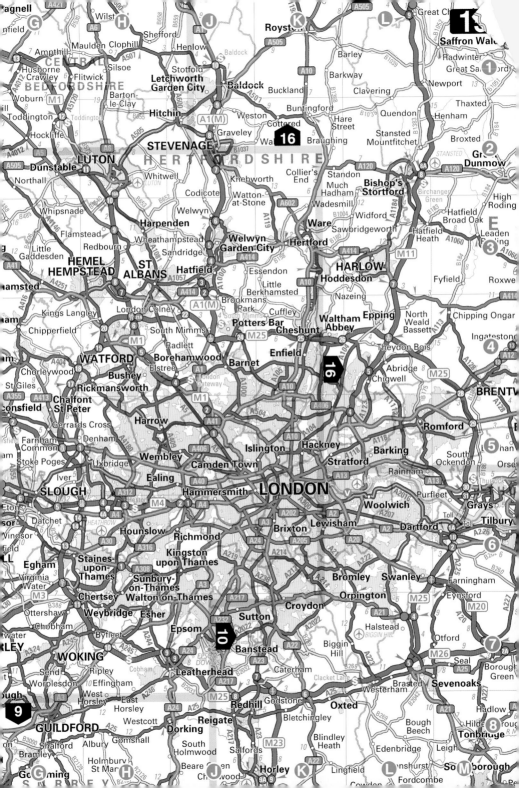

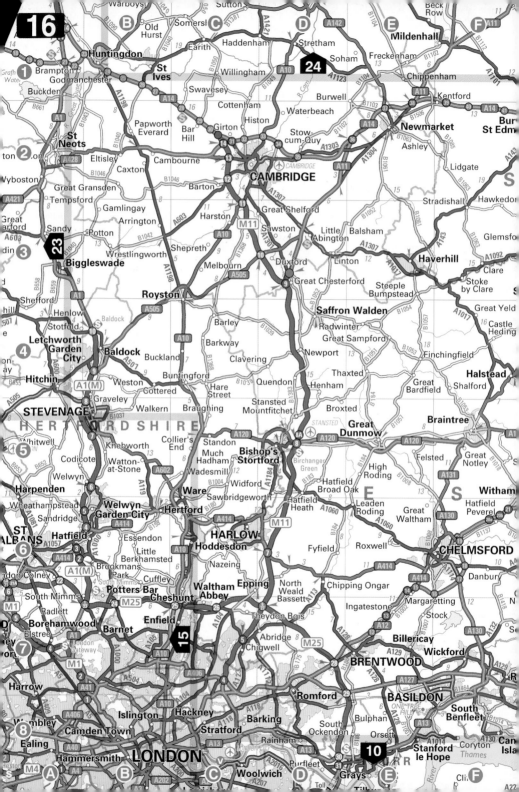

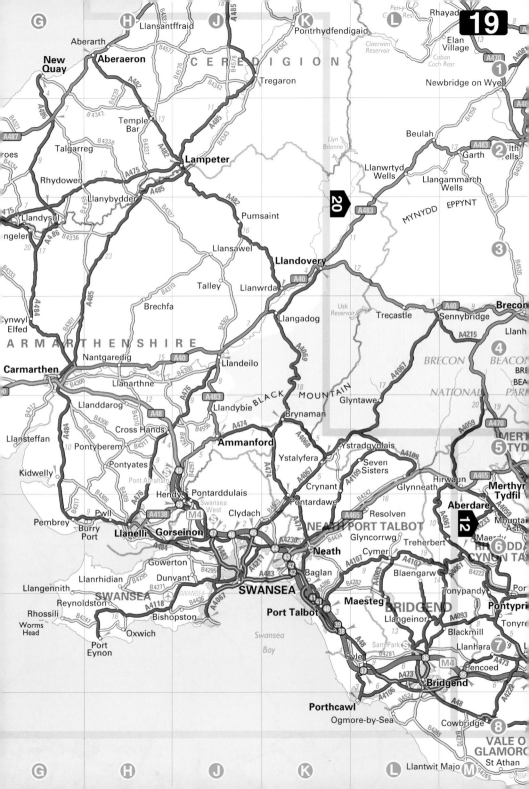

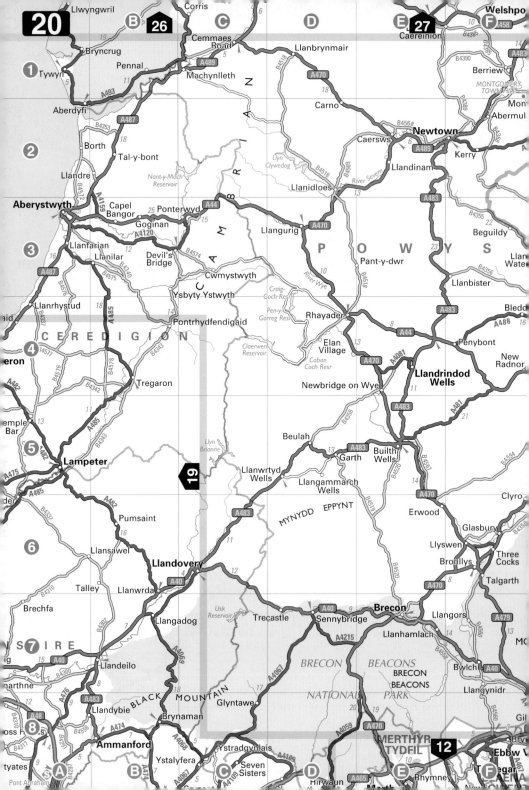

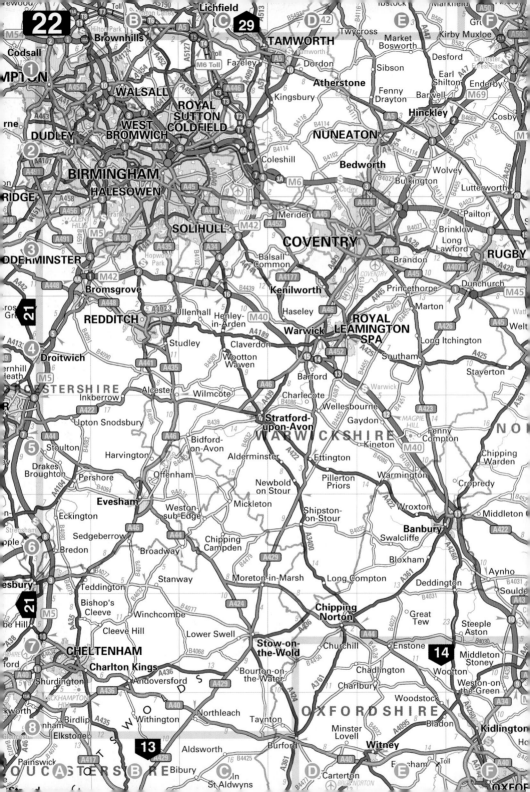

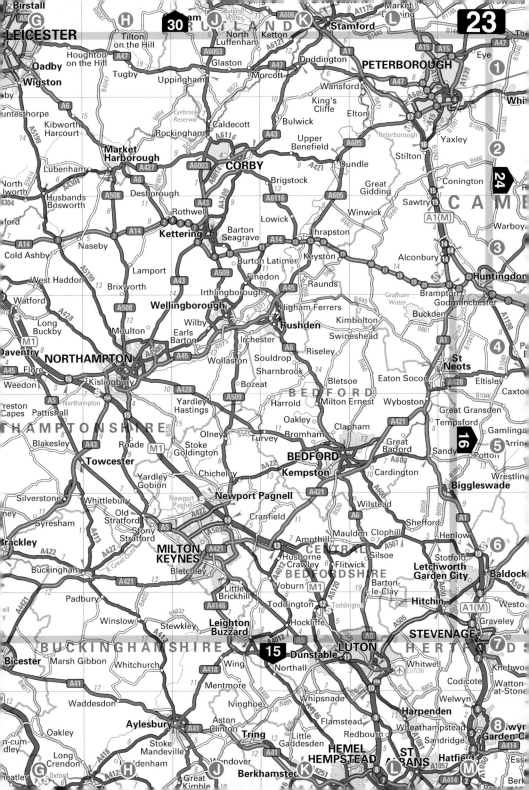

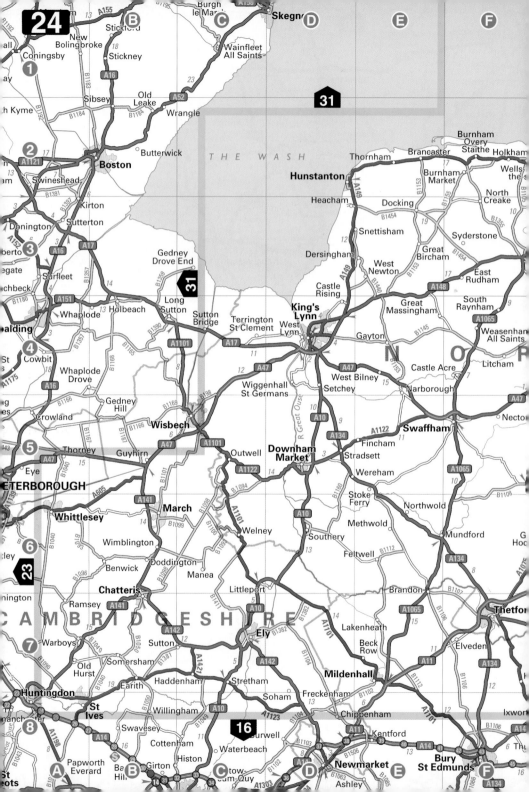

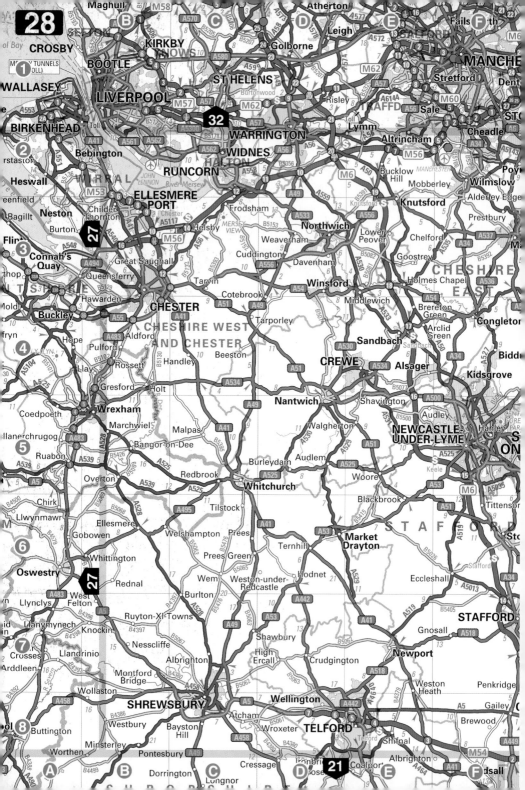

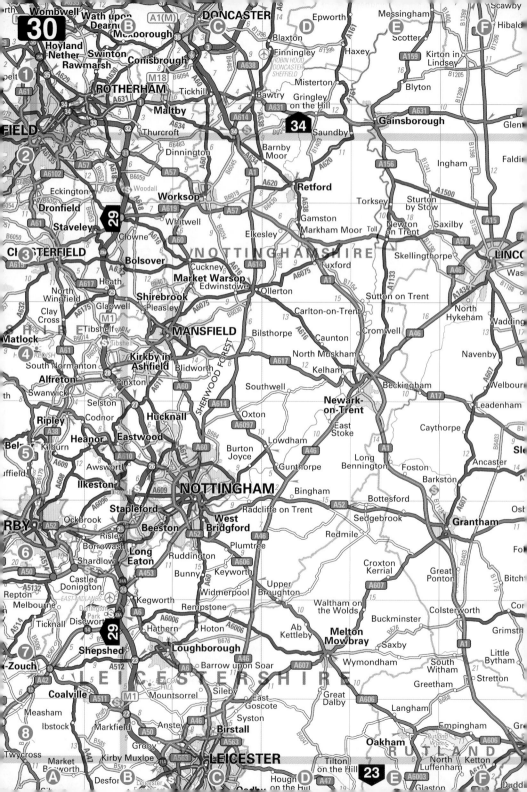

B   C   Maryp D   E   F

41

1   Botel   Ireby   Oxdale
Dearham
Flimby   A594   7   A595   A591
Standingstone   A596   Cockermouth   Bassenthwaite
Workington   Brigham   Bassenthwaite   931   Mu
A66   Lake   SKIDDAW
A597   9   B5292   Portinscale   A66   A591   Threlke
Branthwaite   Braithwaite   Keswick
A595   4   16   Loweswater   Derwent   Grange   Thirlme
A5086   LAKE   Water
2   Whitehaven   Frizington   Ennerdale   Crummock   C
B5295   Bridge   Buttermere   Water   Grange
St Bees   Cleator   Ennerdale   NATIONAL   PAR
Head   Moor   Water   LAKE   DI
B5345   St Bees   Wasdale   899
Head   GREAT GABLE   Great
3   Calder Bridge   6   Nether   978   Langdale
Wasdale   SCAFELL   Elterwa
Wast   PIKE
B5343   Gosforth   Water
Seascale   Eskdale   Boot
Holmrook   Green
Ravenglass   13   Seathwaite   Coniston
A595   Ulpha   Torver   9
4   Bootle   Broughton-   A593   A5084
in-Furness   11
11   A5092
Millom   A595   Greenod
8   7   A595   Ulverston
Askam   5   A590
in Furness   Bardsea
Dalton-in-Furness   Baycliff   13
BARROW-   A5087
IN-FURNESS

Isle of Man

1   miles
0   5   10
0   5   10   15
kilometres

Point
of Ayre
A10
Jurby   Bride
St Jude's   Andreas   A17
2   Sulby   Ramsey
Ballaugh   Maughold
Kirk Michael   I S L E
SNAEFELL
O F   The
Bungalow
Peel   M A N   Laxey
St John's   A1
Patrick   Glen   Crosby   A22
3   Maye   Foxdale
Dalby   A3   Onchan
St   DOUGLAS
Mark's
4   Port Erin   Ballasalla   Douglas
Cregneash   Derbyhaven
Port   Castletown
St Mary
Calf of Man   ISLE OF MAN
(RONALDSWAY)

a   b   c   d

Belfast
Isle of
Walney   Rampside

Heysham   Douglas

Liverpool
Birkenhead
Dublin

8   Fleetw
Clevele
Poulton-
A   B   C   D   E   F   BLACKPO

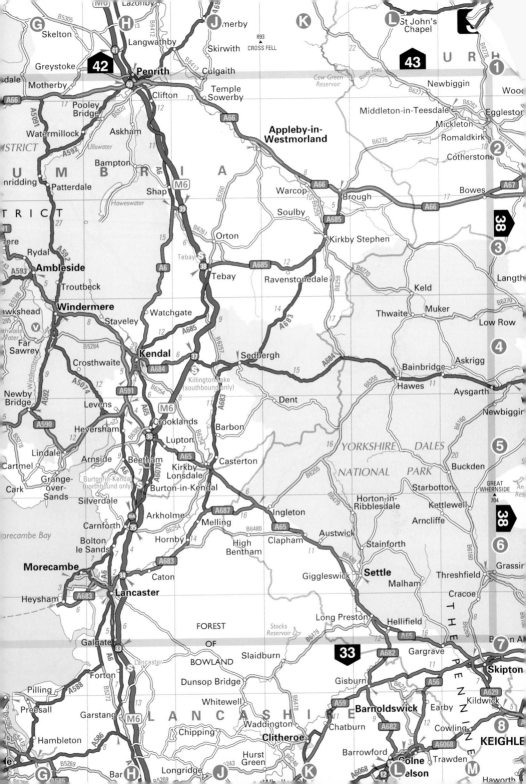

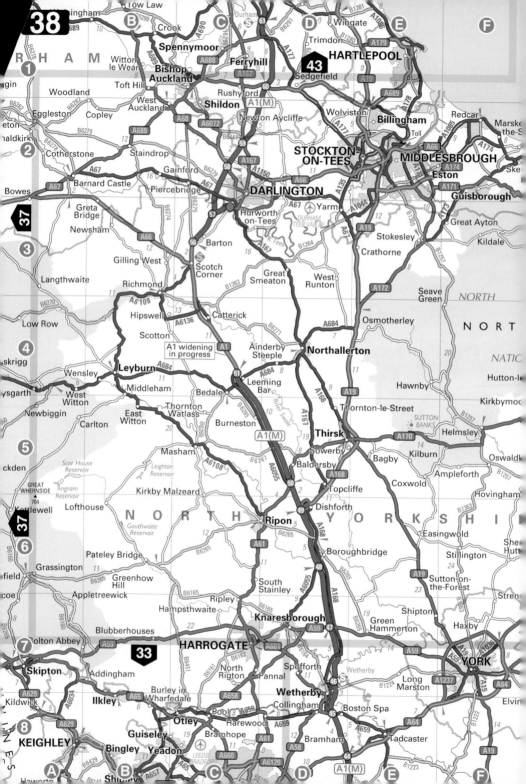

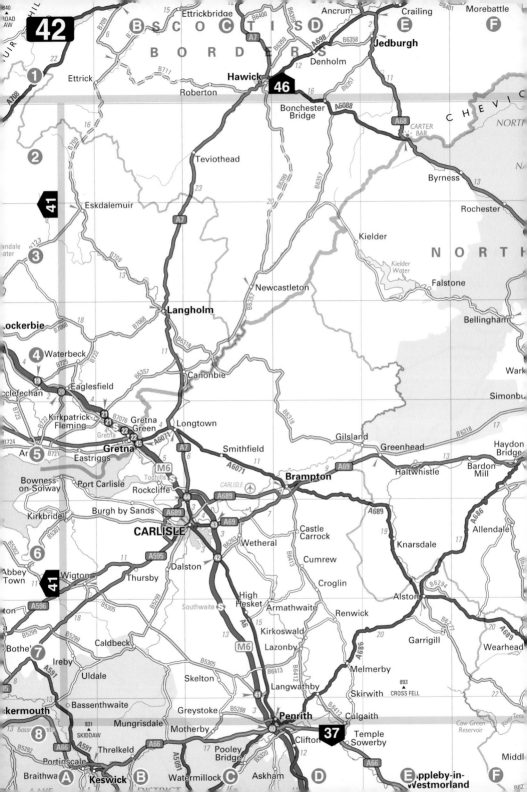

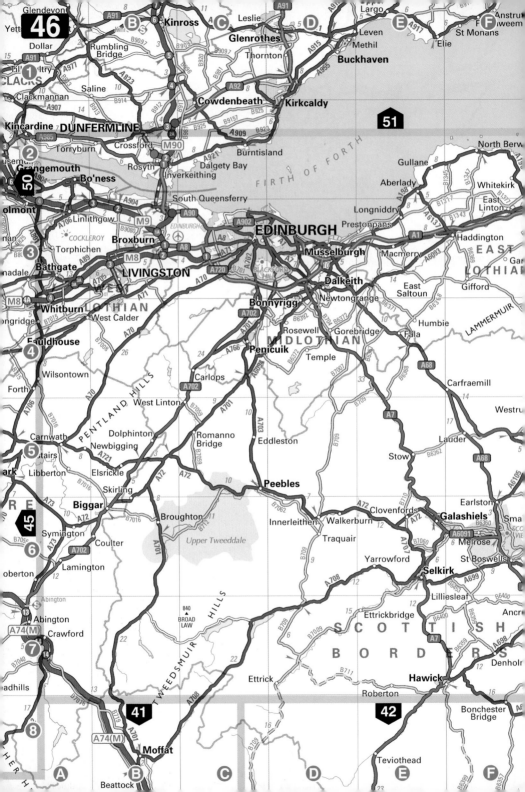

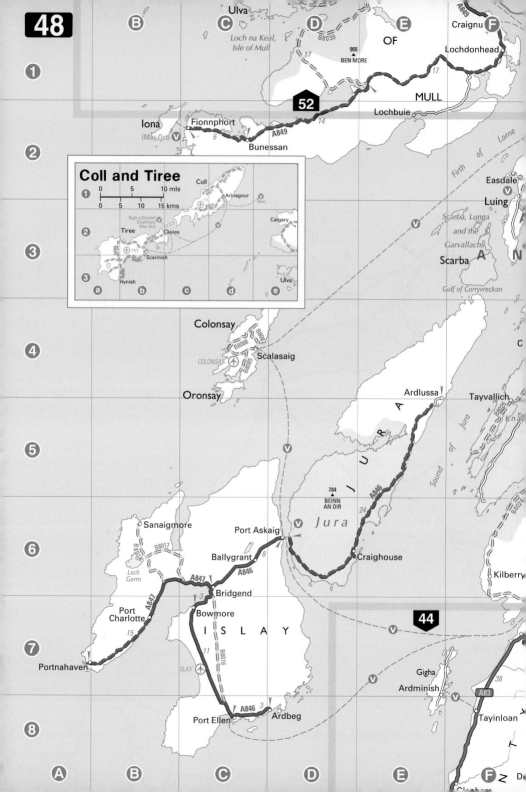

48

Ulva
Loch na Keal,
Isle of Mull
BEN MORE 966
OF
MULL
Craignu
Lochdonhead
A849
B8035
17
17
52
Lochbuie
14
Iona
(Mar-Oct)
Fionnphort
A849
6
Bunessan
Firth of Lorne
Firth of Lorne
Easdale
Luing
Scarba, Lunga
and the
Garvallachs
Scarba
A
N

Coll and Tiree

| 0 | 5 | 10 mls |
| 0 | 5 | 10 | 15 kms |

Coll
Arinagour
Dùn
Bagh a Chaisteil
(Castlebay)
(Mar-Oct)
Tiree
Caoles
Calgary
TIREE
Scarinish
Hynish
Ulva
a   b   c   d   e

Colonsay
B8087
B8086
COLONSAY
B8085
Scalasaig
Ardlussa
Tayvallich
J U R A
Oronsay
Gulf of Corryvreckan
Sound of Jura
B8025
Kn

784
BEINN
AN OIR
A846
24
Sanaigmore
Port Askaig
B8018
B8017
Ballygrant
8
V Jura
Loch
Gorm
A846
Craighouse
Kilberry
A847
Bridgend
Port
Charlotte
A847
3
Bowmore
I S L A Y
B8016
44
Portnahaven
15
11
ISLAY
Gigha
Ardminish
A83
38
Port Ellen
A846
3
Ardbeg
Tayinloan
A B C D E F Z

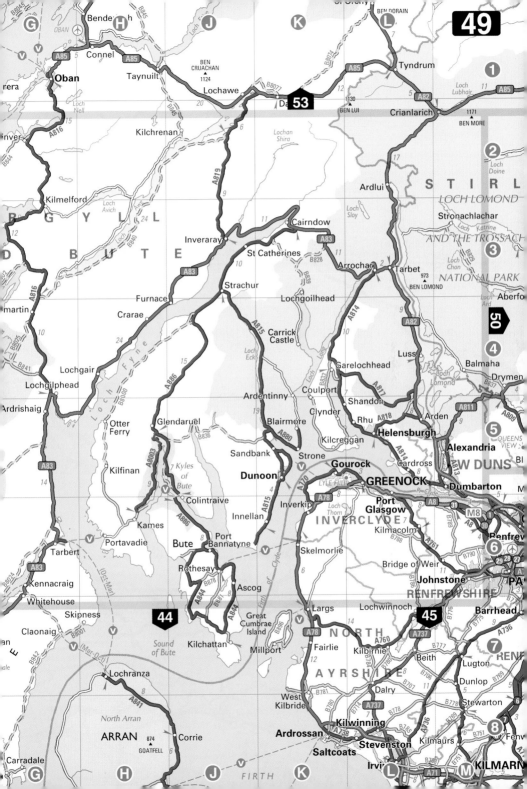

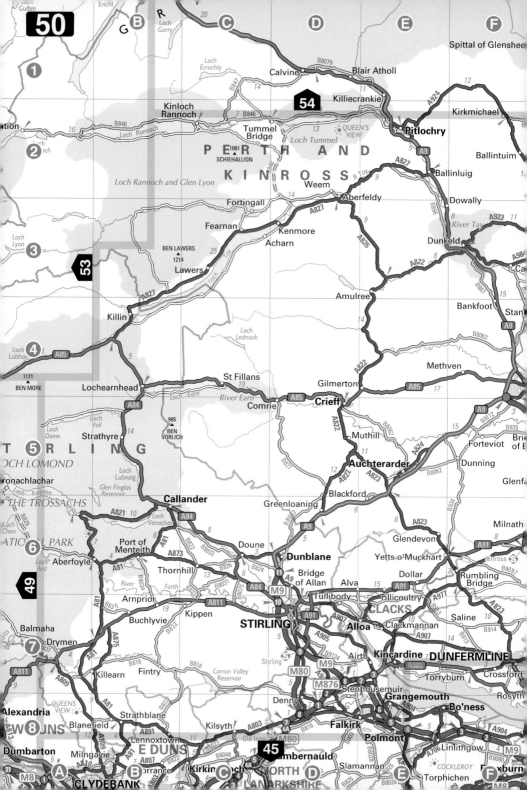

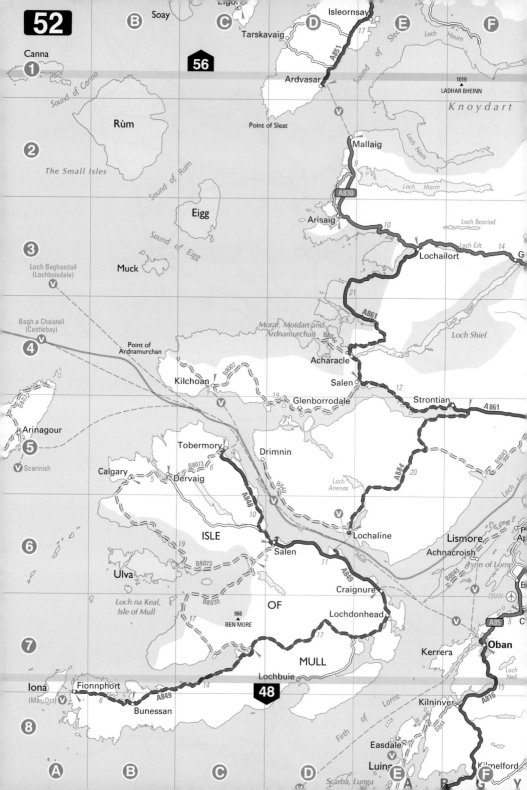

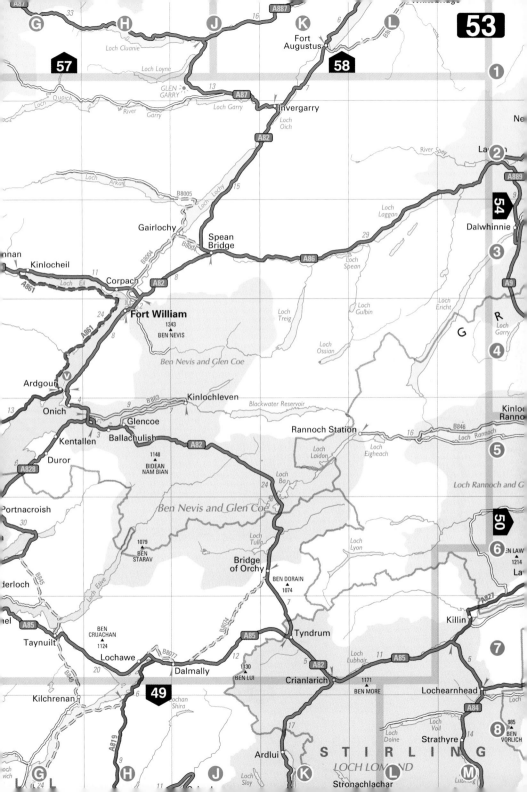

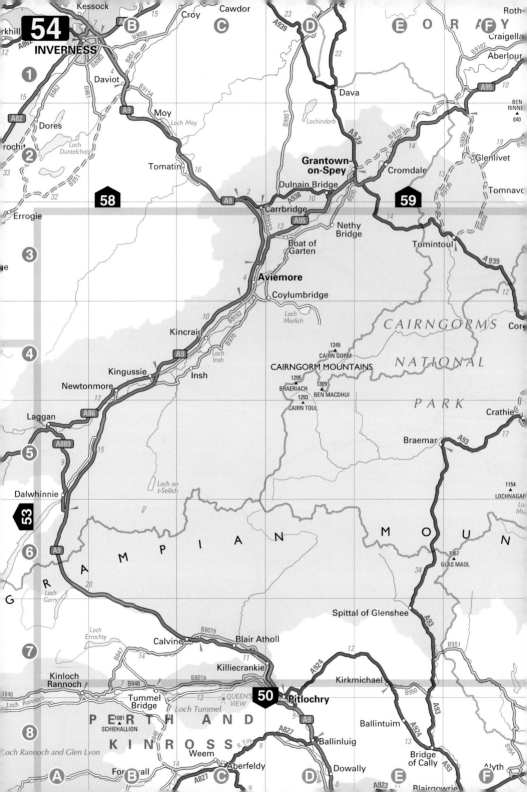

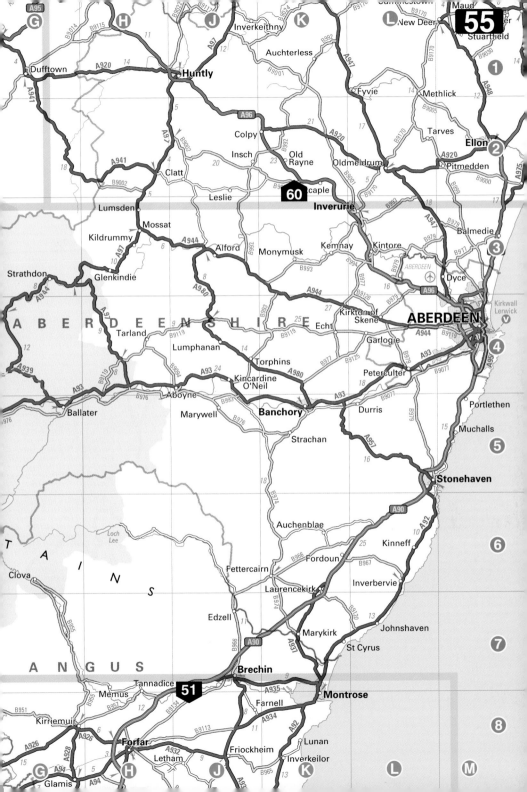

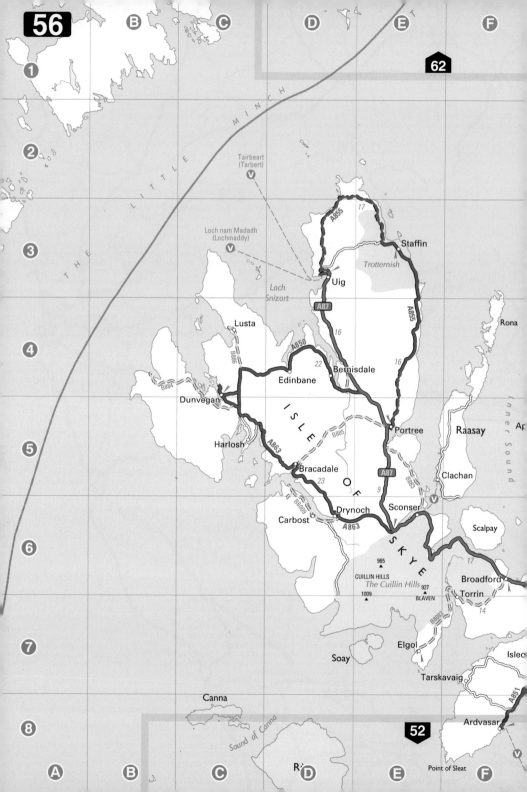

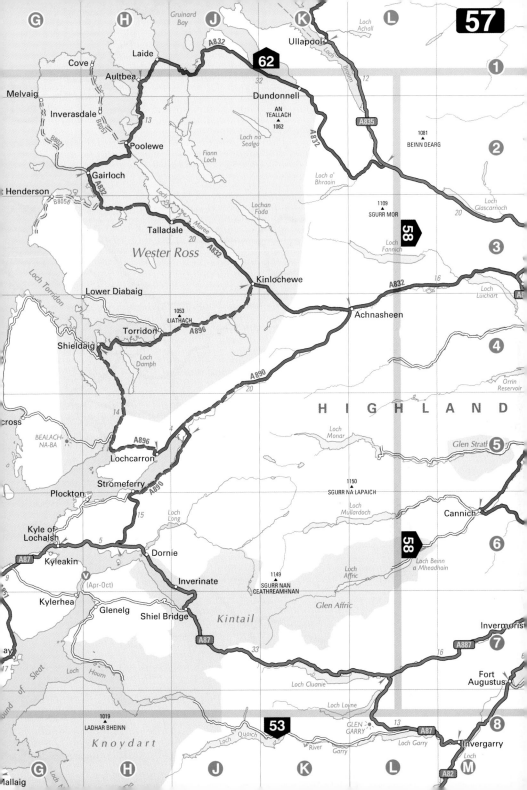

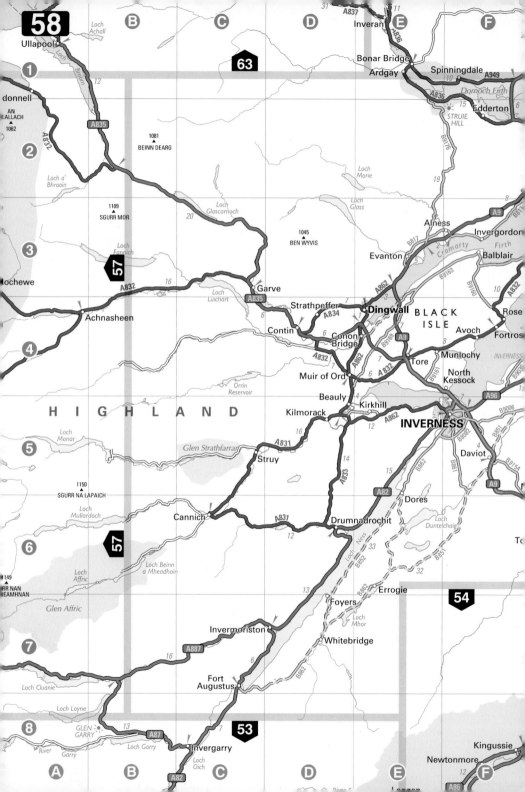

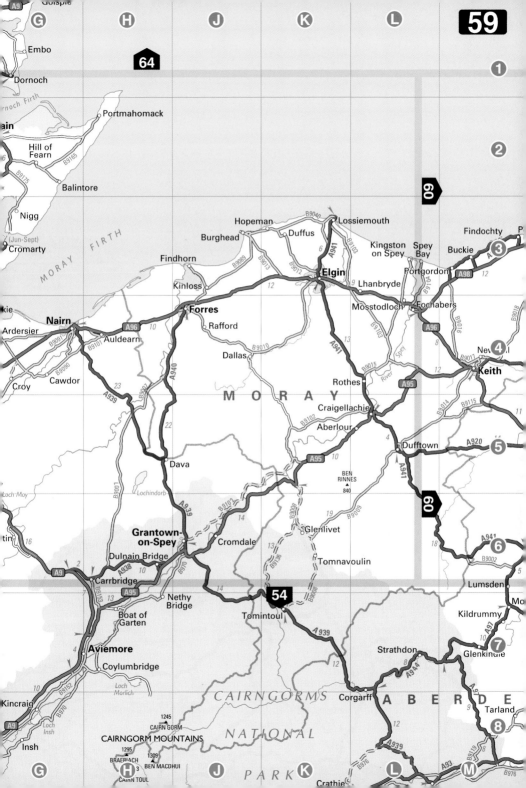

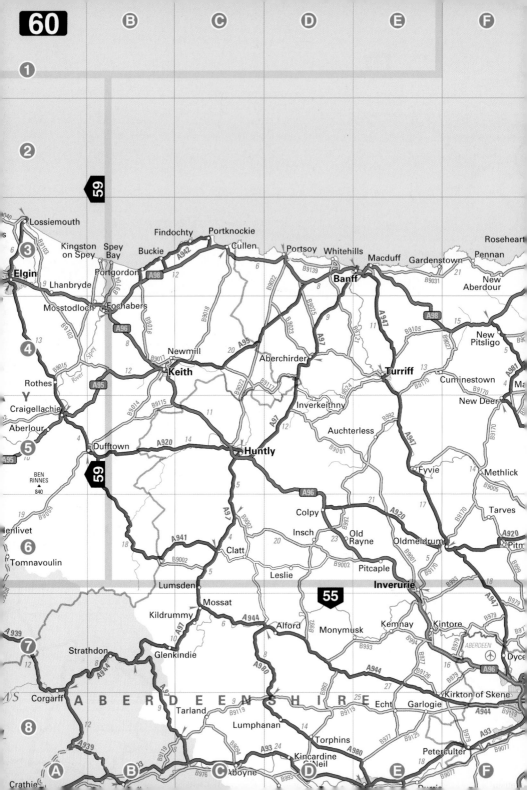

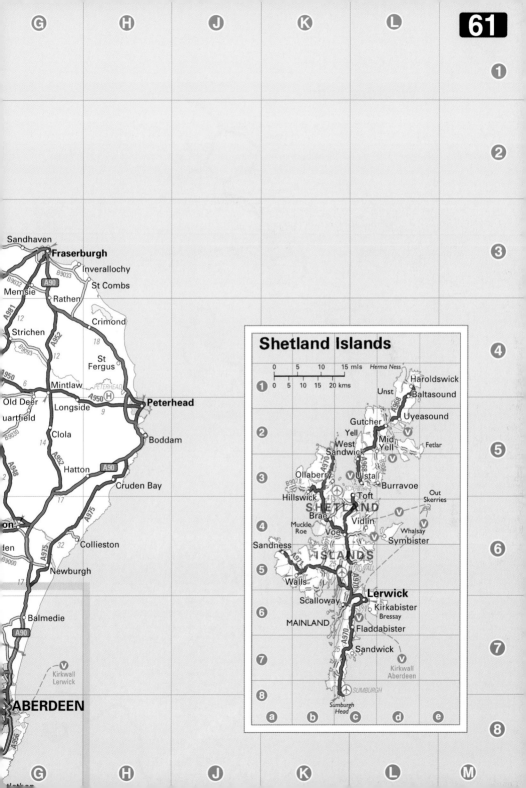

Sandhaven
Fraserburgh
Inverallochy
St Combs
Memsie
Rathen
Crimond
Strichen
St Fergus
Mintlaw
Old Deer
uartfield
Longside
Peterhead
Clola
Boddam
Hatton
Cruden Bay
Collieston
Newburgh
Balmedie
Kirkwall
Lerwick
ABERDEEN

Shetland Islands

0   5   10   15 mls   Herma Ness
0   5   10   15   20 kms

Haroldswick
Unst
Baltasound
Gutcher
Uyeasound
Yell
West Sandwick
Mid Yell
Fetlar
Ollaberry
Ulsta
Burravoe
Hillswick
Toft
Out Skerries
Brae
Muckle Roe
Vidlin
Voe
Whalsay
Sandness
Symbister
ISLANDS
Walls
Lerwick
Scalloway
Kirkabister
Bressay
MAINLAND
Fladdabister
Sandwick
Kirkwall
Aberdeen
Sumburgh
Sumburgh Head

SHETLAND

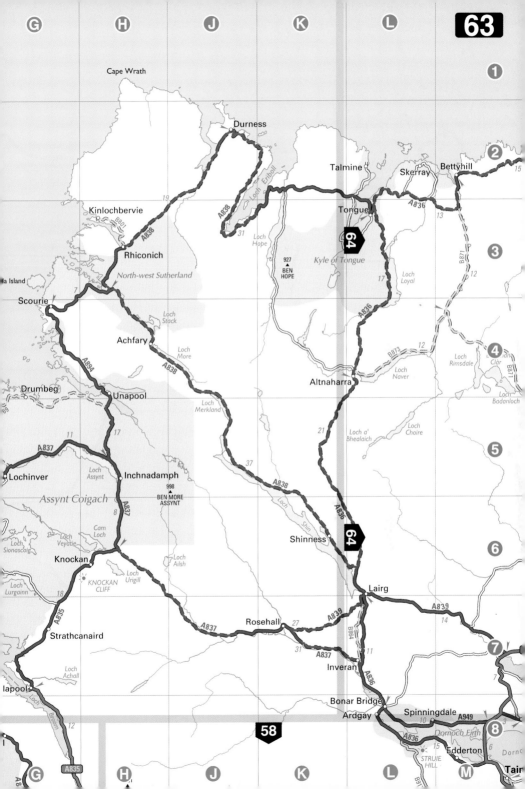

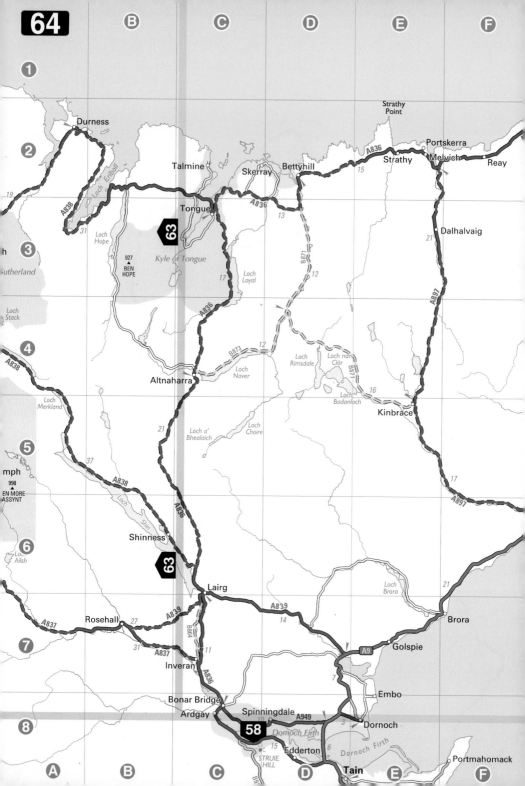

Index to places in Britain

This index lists places appearing in the main-map section of the atlas in alphabetical order. The reference following each name gives the atlas page number and grid reference of the square in which the place appears. The map shows counties, unitary authorities and administrative areas, together with a list of the abbreviated name forms used in the index.

England

BaNES	**Bath & N E Somerset (18)**
Barns	**Barnsley (19)**
Bed	**Bedford**
Birm	**Birmingham**
Bl w D	**Blackburn with Darwen (20)**
Bmouth	**Bournemouth**
Bolton	**Bolton (21)**
Bpool	**Blackpool**
Br & H	**Brighton & Hove (22)**
Br For	**Bracknell Forest (23)**
Bristl	**City of Bristol**
Bucks	**Buckinghamshire**
Bury	**Bury (24)**
C Beds	**Central Bedfordshire**
C Brad	**City of Bradford**
C Derb	**City of Derby**
C KuH	**City of Kingston upon Hull**
C Leic	**City of Leicester**
C Nott	**City of Nottingham**
C Pete	**City of Peterborough**
C Plym	**City of Plymouth**
C Port	**City of Portsmouth**
C Sotn	**City of Southampton**
C Stke	**City of Stoke-on-Trent**
C York	**City of York**
Calder	**Calderdale (25)**
Cambs	**Cambridgeshire**
Ches E	**Cheshire East**
Ches W	**Cheshire West and Chester**
Cnwll	**Cornwall**
Covtry	**Coventry**
Cumb	**Cumbria**
Darltn	**Darlington (26)**
Derbys	**Derbyshire**
Devon	**Devon**
Donc	**Doncaster (27)**
Dorset	**Dorset**
Dudley	**Dudley (28)**
Dur	**Durham**
E R Yk	**East Riding of Yorkshire**
E Susx	**East Sussex**
Essex	**Essex**
Gatesd	**Gateshead (29)**
Gloucs	**Gloucestershire**
Gt Lon	**Greater London**
Halton	**Halton (30)**
Hants	**Hampshire**
Hartpl	**Hartlepool (31)**
Herefs	**Herefordshire**
Herts	**Hertfordshire**
IoS	**Isles of Scilly**
IoW	**Isle of Wight**
Kent	**Kent**
Kirk	**Kirklees (32)**
Knows	**Knowsley (33)**
Lancs	**Lancashire**
Leeds	**Leeds**
Leics	**Leicestershire**
Lincs	**Lincolnshire**
Lpool	**Liverpool**
Luton	**Luton**
M Keyn	**Milton Keynes**
Manch	**Manchester**
Medway	**Medway**
Middsb	**Middlesbrough**
NE Lin	**North East Lincolnshire**
N Linc	**North Lincolnshire**
N Som	**North Somerset (34)**
N Tyne	**North Tyneside (35)**
N u Ty	**Newcastle upon Tyne**
N York	**North Yorkshire**
Nhants	**Northamptonshire**
Norfk	**Norfolk**
Notts	**Nottinghamshire**
Nthumb	**Northumberland**
Oldham	**Oldham (36)**
Oxon	**Oxfordshire**
Poole	**Poole**
R & Cl	**Redcar & Cleveland**
Readg	**Reading**
Rochdl	**Rochdale (37)**
Rothm	**Rotherham (38)**
Rutlnd	**Rutland**
S Glos	**South Gloucestershire (39)**
S on T	**Stockton-on-Tees (40)**
S Tyne	**South Tyneside (41)**
Salfd	**Salford (42)**
Sandw	**Sandwell (43)**
Sefton	**Sefton (44)**
Sheff	**Sheffield**
Shrops	**Shropshire**
Slough	**Slough (45)**
Solhll	**Solihull (46)**
Somset	**Somerset**
St Hel	**St Helens (47)**
Staffs	**Staffordshire**
Sthend	**Southend-on-Sea**
Stockp	**Stockport (48)**
Suffk	**Suffolk**
Sundld	**Sunderland**
Surrey	**Surrey**
Swindn	**Swindon**
Tamesd	**Tameside (49)**
Thurr	**Thurrock (50)**
Torbay	**Torbay**
Traffd	**Trafford (51)**
W & M	**Windsor and Maidenhead (52)**
W Berk	**West Berkshire**
W Susx	**West Sussex**
Wakefd	**Wakefield (53)**
Warrtn	**Warrington (54)**
Warwks	**Warwickshire**
Wigan	**Wigan (55)**
Wilts	**Wiltshire**
Wirral	**Wirral (56)**
Wokham	**Wokingham (57)**
Wolves	**Wolverhampton (58)**
Worcs	**Worcestershire**
Wrekin	**Telford & Wrekin (59)**
Wsall	**Walsall (60)**

Channel Islands & Isle of Man

Guern	**Guernsey**
Jersey	**Jersey**
IoM	**Isle of Man**

Scotland

Abers	**Aberdeenshire**
Ag & B	**Argyll and Bute**
Angus	**Angus**
Border	**Scottish Borders**
C Aber	**City of Aberdeen**
C Dund	**City of Dundee**
C Edin	**City of Edinburgh**
C Glas	**City of Glasgow**
Clacks	**Clackmannanshire (1)**
D & G	**Dumfries & Galloway**
E Ayrs	**East Ayrshire**
E Duns	**East Dunbartonshire (2)**
E Loth	**East Lothian**
E Rens	**East Renfrewshire (3)**
Falk	**Falkirk**
Fife	**Fife**
Highld	**Highland**
Inver	**Inverclyde (4)**
Mdloth	**Midlothian (5)**
Moray	**Moray**
N Ayrs	**North Ayrshire**
N Lans	**North Lanarkshire (6)**
Ork	**Orkney Islands**
P & K	**Perth & Kinross**
Rens	**Renfrewshire (7)**
S Ayrs	**South Ayrshire**
Shet	**Shetland Islands**
S Lans	**South Lanarkshire**
Stirlg	**Stirling**
W Duns	**West Dunbartonshire (8)**
W Isls	**Western Isles (Na h-Eileanan an Iar)**
W Loth	**West Lothian**

Wales

Blae G	**Blaenau Gwent (9)**
Brdgnd	**Bridgend (10)**
Caerph	**Caerphilly (11)**
Cardif	**Cardiff**
Carmth	**Carmarthenshire**
Cerdgn	**Ceredigion**
Conwy	**Conwy**
Denbgs	**Denbighshire**
Flints	**Flintshire**
Gwynd	**Gwynedd**
IoA	**Isle of Anglesey**
Mons	**Monmouthshire**
Myr Td	**Merthyr Tydfil (12)**
Neath	**Neath Port Talbot (13)**
Newpt	**Newport (14)**
Pembks	**Pembrokeshire**
Powys	**Powys**
Rhondd	**Rhondda Cynon Taff (15)**
Swans	**Swansea**
Torfn	**Torfaen (16)**
V Glam	**Vale of Glamorgan (17)**
Wrexhm	**Wrexham**

ORKNEY
ISLANDS

SHETLAND
ISLANDS

WESTERN ISLES (Na h-Eileanan an Iar)

HIGHLAND

MORAY

S C O T L A N D

Aberdeen

ABERDEENSHIRE

ANGUS

PERTH &
KINROSS

Dundee

ARGYLL
& BUTE

STIRLING

FIFE

1

8   2   FALK
4   Glasgow   6   W   Edinburgh
7   3   LOTH   E LOTH
5

NORTH
AYRSHIRE

S LANS

SCOTTISH
BORDERS

E AYRS

S AYRS

DUMFRIES &
GALLOWAY

NORTHUMBERLAND

Newcastle
upon Tyne   35
29   41
Sunderland

CUMBRIA

DURHAM

31

26   40   R & CL
Middlesbrough

IoM

NORTH YORKSHIRE

Blackpool

LANCASHIRE

Bradford

York

EAST RIDING
OF YORKSHIRE

Leeds

Kingston
upon Hull

20   25   53   N LINC   N E
LIN

44   55   21 24 37   36   32   19   27
47   42   49
Liverpool   33   51   Manchester   38
56   30   54   48   Sheffield

IoA

CONWY   FLINTS   CHES
W   CHES
E   DERBYS   NOTTS   LINCOLNSHIRE

DENBGS   Stoke-on-
Trent   Nottingham

GWYNEDD   WREXHAM   Derby

STAFFS   DERBYS

59   LEICS   RUTLAND   NORFOLK

SHROPSHIRE   58 60   Leicester   Peterborough
28 43   Birmingham
46   Coventry   CAMBS

POWYS   NHANTS   SUFFOLK

CERDGN   WORCS   WARWKS   Milton
Keynes   BED

HEREFS   BEDS   Luton   ESSEX

PEMBKS   CARMTH   GLOUCS   HERTS

13   12   9   MONS   OXON   BUCKS   Southend-
16   on-Sea
10   11   BUCKS   GREATER
Swansea   14   Bristol   39   Swindon   Reading   52   45   LONDON   50
15   Cardiff   W BERK   23   MEDWAY
17   34   18   57   SURREY

W A L E S   E N G L A N D   WILTSHIRE   KENT

SOMERSET   HAMPSHIRE   W SUSX   E SUSX   22

DEVON   DORSET   Southampton
Bournemouth   Portsmouth
Poole   IoW

CORNWALL   Plymouth   Torbay   CHANNEL
ISLANDS   Guernsey
Jersey

IoS

A

Abberley Worcs	21	L4
Abbey Town Cumb	41	L6
Abbots Bromley		
Staffs	29	H7
Aberaeron Cerdgn	19	H1
Aberarth Cerdgn	19	H1
Aberchirder Abers	60	D4
Aberdare Rhondd	12	B2
Aberdaron Gwynd	26	B6
Aberdeen C Aber	55	M4
Aberdyfi Gwynd	20	A2
Aberfeldy P & K	50	D2
Aberffraw IoA	26	C3
Aberfoyle Stirlg	50	B6
Abergavenny Mons	21	G8
Abergele Conwy	27	H3
Aberlady E Loth	46	E2
Aberlour Moray	59	L5
Abermule Powys	20	F2
Abernethy P & K	51	G5
Aberporth Cerdgn	18	F2
Abersoch Gwynd	26	C6
Abersychan Torfn	12	D2
Abertillery Blae G	12	D2
Aberystwyth Cerdgn	20	A3
Abingdon-on-		
Thames Oxon	14	C4
Abington S Lans	45	M5
Ab Kettleby Leics	30	D7
Aboyne Abers	55	J4
Abridge Essex	16	D7
Accrington Lancs	33	G4
Acharacle Highld	52	D4
Acharn P & K	50	C3
Achfary Highld	63	H4
Achiltibuie Highld	62	F6
Achnacroish Ag & B	52	F6
Achnasheen Highld	57	L4
Ackworth Moor Top		
Wakefd	34	B5
Acle Norfk	25	K5
Acton Trussell Staffs	29	G7
Addingham C Brad	33	J2
Adwick Le Street		
Donc	34	C6
Ainderby Steeple		
N York	38	D4
Airdrie N Lans	45	L2
Airth Falk	50	E7
Albrighton Shrops	21	L1
Albrighton Shrops	28	C7
Albury Surrey	9	K2
Alcester Warwks	22	B4
Alconbury Cambs	23	M3
Aldbourne Wilts	14	A6
Aldbrough E R Yk	35	J3
Aldeburgh Suffk	17	M2
Alderbury Wilts	8	C3
Alderley Edge Ches E	28	E4
Aldermaston W Berk	14	D7
Alderminster Warwks	22	D5
Aldershot Hants	9	H2
Aldford Ches W	28	B4
Aldham Essex	17	G5
Aldsworth Gloucs	13	L1
Alexandria W Duns	49	M5
Alfold Surrey	9	K3
Alford Abers	55	J3
Alford Lincs	31	K3
Alfreton Derbys	29	L4
Alfriston E Susx	10	D7
Alkham Kent	11	K4
Allanton Border	47	H4
Allendale Nthumb	42	F6
Allenheads Nthumb	42	F7
Allensmore Herefs	21	J6
Alloa Clacks	50	E7
Allonby Cumb	41	L7
Alloway S Ayrs	45	G6
Almondsbury S Glos	13	G3
Alness Highld	58	F3
Alnmouth Nthumb	43	K2
Alnwick Nthumb	47	L7
Alrewas Staffs	29	J7
Alsager Ches E	28	E4
Alston Cumb	42	E6
Altandhu Highld	62	F6
Althorpe N Linc	34	E5
Altnaharra Highld	64	C4
Alton Hants	9	G2
Alton Pancras Dorset	7	K2
Altrincham Traffd	28	E2
Alva Clacks	50	E6
Alveston S Glos	13	G3
Alyth P & K	51	G3
Amberley W Susx	9	K4
Amble Nthumb	43	K2
Ambleside Cumb	37	G3

Amersham Bucks	15	G4
Amesbury Wilts	8	C2
Amlwch IoA	26	D1
Ammanford Carmth	19	J5
Ampleforth N York	38	F5
Ampthill C Beds	23	K6
Amroth Pembks	18	E5
Amulree P & K	50	E3
Ancaster Lincs	30	F5
Ancroft Nthumb	47	K5
Ancrum Border	47	G7
Andover Hants	8	D2
Andoversford Gloucs	22	B7
Andreas IoM	36	c1
Angle Pembks	18	C6
Angmering W Susx	9	K5
Annan D & G	41	M5
Annfield Plain Dur	43	J6
Anstey Leics	30	C8
Anstruther Fife	51	K6
An t-Ob W Isls	62	e7
Anwick Lincs	31	G5
Appleby-in-		
Westmorland		
Cumb	37	J2
Applecross Highld	57	G5
Appledore Devon	4	D4
Appledore Kent	11	H5
Appletreewick		
N York	38	A7
Arbroath Angus	51	L3
Arclid Green Ches E	28	E4
Ardbeg Ag & B	48	D8
Arddleen Powys	27	L7
Arden Ag & B	49	L5
Ardentinny Ag & B	49	K4
Ardersier Highld	59	G4
Ardgay Highld	64	C8
Ardgour Highld	52	F4
Ardingly W Susx	10	C5
Ardleigh Essex	17	H4
Ardlui Ag & B	49	L2
Ardlussa Ag & B	48	E4
Ardminish Ag & B	44	A3
Ardrishaig Ag & B	49	G5
Ardrossan N Ayrs	44	F4
Ardvasar Highld	52	D1
Ardwell D & G	40	C7
Arinagour Ag & B	48	d1
Arisaig Highld	52	D3
Arkholme Lancs	37	J6
Armadale W Loth	45	M2
Armathwaite Cumb	42	C7
Arncliffe N York	37	M6
Arnprior Stirlg	50	B7
Arnside Cumb	37	H5
Arrington Cambs	16	B3
Arrochar Ag & B	49	L3
Arundel W Susx	9	K5
Ascog Ag & B	49	J6
Ascot W & M	15	G6
Ash Kent	11	K3
Ashbourne Derbys	29	J5
Ashburton Devon	6	B7
Ashbury Oxon	14	A5
Ashby-de-la-Zouch		
Leics	29	K7
Ashcott Somset	12	E7
Ashford Kent	11	H4
Ashington Nthumb	43	K3
Ashington W Susx	9	L4
Ashley Cambs	16	E2
Ashton-under-Lyne		
Tamesd	33	H4
Ashurst Hants	8	D5
Ashwater Devon	4	D7
Askam in Furness		
Cumb	36	F5
Askern Donc	34	C5
Askham Cumb	37	H2
Askrigg N York	37	M4
Aspatria Cumb	41	L7
Aston Oxon	14	B4
Aston Clinton Bucks	14	F3
Aston on Clun Shrops	21	H3
Aston Rowant Oxon	14	E4
Atcham Shrops	28	C8
Atherstone Warwks	22	F2
Atherton Wigan	32	F6
Attleborough Norfk	25	H4
Attlebridge Norfk	25	H4
Atwick E R Yk	35	J2
Auchenblae Abers	55	K6
Auchencairn D & G	41	H6
Auchinleck E Ayrs	45	J5
Auchterarder P & K	50	E5
Auchterless Abers	60	E5
Auchtermuchty Fife	51	G5
Audlem Ches E	28	D5
Audley Staffs	28	E5
Auldearn Highld	59	H4

Auldgirth D & G	41	J3
Aultbea Highld	57	H1
Austwick N York	37	K6
Avebury Wilts	13	L4
Avening Gloucs	13	J2
Aveton Gifford		
Devon	6	A6
Aviemore Highld	54	C3
Avoch Highld	58	F4
Avonmouth Bristl	12	F4
Awsworth Notts	30	B5
Axbridge Somset	12	E5
Axminster Devon	6	F3
Axmouth Devon	6	F3
Aylesbury Bucks	14	F3
Aylesham Kent	11	K3
Aylsham Norfk	25	J3
Aynho Nhants	22	F6
Ayr S Ayrs	45	G5
Aysgarth N York	38	A4
Ayton Border	47	J4

B

Backaland Ork	65	d2
Bacton Norfk	25	K3
Bacup Lancs	33	H4
Bagby N York	38	E5
Bagh a Chaisteil W Isls	62	b14
Bagillt Flints	27	K3
Baglan Neath	19	K6
Bagshot Surrey	14	F7
Baile Ailein W Isls	62	g4
Baile a Mhanaich		
W Isls	62	c10
Bainbridge N York	37	M4
Bainton E R Yk	34	F2
Bakewell Derbys	29	J3
Bala Gwynd	27	H6
Balallan W Isls	62	g4
Balbeggie P & K	51	G4
Balblair Highld	58	F3
Balcombe W Susx	10	B5
Baldersby N York	38	D5
Baldock Herts	16	B4
Balfour Ork	65	c3
Balintore Highld	59	G2
Balivanich W Isls	62	c10
Ballachulish Highld	53	H5
Ballantrae S Ayrs	40	B4
Ballasalla IoM	36	b4
Ballater Abers	55	G5
Ballaugh IoM	36	c2
Ballinluig P & K	50	E2
Ballintuim P & K	50	F2
Ballygrant Ag & B	48	C6
Balmaclellan D & G	41	G4
Balmaha Stirlg	49	M4
Balmedie Abers	55	M3
Balsall Common		
Solhll	22	D3
Balsham Cambs	16	E3
Baltasound Shet	61	d1
Bamber Bridge Lancs	32	E4
Bamburgh Nthumb	47	L6
Bamford Derbys	29	J2
Bampton Cumb	37	H2
Bampton Devon	5	H5
Bampton Oxon	14	A4
Banbury Oxon	22	E6
Banchory Abers	55	K5
Banff Abers	60	E3
Bangor Gwynd	26	E3
Bangor-on-Dee		
Wrexhm	28	B5
Banham Norfk	25	H6
Bankfoot P & K	50	F4
Banstead Surrey	10	B3
Banwell N Som	12	E5
Barabhas W Isls	62	h2
Barbon Cumb	37	J5
Bardney Lincs	31	G3
Bardon Mill Nthumb	42	F5
Bardsea Cumb	36	F5
Barford Warwks	22	D4
Bargoed Caerph	12	C2
Bar Hill Cambs	16	C2
Barkby Leics	30	C8
Barkston Lincs	30	F5
Barkway Herts	16	C4
Barley Herts	16	C4
Barmby Moor E R Yk	34	E2
Barmouth Gwynd	26	E7
Barmston E R Yk	35	J2
Barnard Castle Dur	38	A2
Barnby Moor Notts	30	D2
Barnet Gt Lon	15	J4
Barnetby le Wold		
N Linc	35	G6

Barnoldswick Lancs	33	H3
Barnsley Barns	33	M6
Barnsley Gloucs	13	L2
Barnstaple Devon	4	E4
Barr S Ayrs	40	D3
Barrasford Nthumb	43	G4
Barrhead E Rens	45	H3
Barrhill S Ayrs	40	D4
Barrowford Lancs	33	H3
Barrow-in-Furness		
Cumb	36	E6
Barrow upon Soar		
Leics	30	C7
Barry V Glam	5	K1
Barton Cambs	16	C2
Barton Lancs	32	E3
Barton N York	38	C3
Barton-le-Clay		
C Beds	23	L7
Barton Seagrave		
Nhants	23	J3
Barton-under-		
Needwood Staffs	29	J7
Barton-upon-		
Humber N Linc	35	G5
Barvas W Isls	62	h2
Barwell Leics	22	E2
Basildon Essex	16	F7
Basingstoke Hants	9	G1
Baslow Derbys	29	J3
Bassenthwaite		
Cumb	42	A8
Baston Lincs	31	G7
Bath BaNES	13	H5
Bathgate W Loth	46	A3
Batley Kirk	33	L4
Battle E Susx	10	F6
Baumber Lincs	31	H3
Bawdeswell Norfk	25	H4
Bawdsey Suffk	17	L4
Bawtry Donc	34	D7
Bayston Hill Shrops	28	C8
Beaconsfield Bucks	15	G5
Beadnell Nthumb	47	L6
Beaford Devon	4	E5
Beal Nthumb	47	K5
Beaminster Dorset	7	H2
Beare Green Surrey	9	L2
Bearsted Kent	10	F3
Beattock D & G	41	L2
Beaulieu Hants	8	E5
Beauly Highld	58	D5
Beaumaris IoA	26	E3
Beaumont Jersey	7	b2
Beaworthy Devon	4	D7
Bebington Wirral	27	L2
Beccles Suffk	25	L6
Beckhampton Wilts	13	L4
Beckingham Lincs	30	E4
Beckington Somset	13	H6
Beck Row Suffk	24	E7
Bedale N York	38	C4
Beddgelert Gwynd	26	E5
Bedford Bed	23	K5
Bedlington Nthumb	43	K4
Bedwas Caerph	12	C3
Bedworth Warwks	22	E2
Beeford E R Yk	35	H2
Beeley Derbys	29	J3
Beer Devon	6	F3
Beesands Devon	6	B7
Beeston Ches W	28	C4
Beeston Notts	30	B6
Beeswing D & G	41	J5
Beetham Cumb	37	H5
Beetley Norfk	25	G4
Beguildy Powys	20	F3
Beith N Ayrs	45	G3
Belford Nthumb	47	L6
Bellingham Nthumb	42	F4
Bellochantuy Ag & B	44	A5
Bellshill N Lans	45	K2
Belper Derbys	29	K5
Belsay Nthumb	43	H4
Belton N Linc	34	E6
Belton Norfk	25	L5
Bembridge IoW	9	G6
Bempton E R Yk	39	L6
Benderloch Ag & B	52	F6
Benenden Kent	10	F5
Benllech IoA	26	D2
Benson Oxon	14	D5
Bentley Hants	9	H2
Benwick Cambs	24	B6
Bere Alston Devon	3	K4
Bere Ferrers Devon	3	K4
Bere Regis Dorset	7	L3
Berkeley Gloucs	13	G2
Berkhamsted Herts	15	G3
Bernisdale Highld	56	D4
Berriedale Highld	65	G6

Berriew Powys............20 F1
Berrow Somset............12 D6
Berwick St John Wilts...13 K8
Berwick-upon-
Tweed Nthumb........47 K4
Bethersden Kent............11 G4
Bethesda Gwynd............26 E3
Bettyhill Highld............64 D2
Betws-y-Coed Conwy...27 G4
Betws-yn-Rhos
Conwy............27 H3
Beulah Powys............20 D5
Beverley E R Yk............35 G3
Bewdley Worcs............21 L3
Bexhill E Susx............10 F7
Bibury Gloucs............13 L1
Bicester Oxon............14 D2
Bickleigh Devon............5 H6
Biddenden Kent............11 G4
Biddisham Somset............12 E6
Biddulph Staffs............28 F4
Bideford Devon............4 D5
Bidford-on-Avon
Warwks............22 C5
Bigbury-on-Sea
Devon............3 M6
Biggar S Lans............46 B6
Biggin Hill Gt Lon............10 C3
Biggleswade C Beds...23 M5
Bildeston Suffk............17 H3
Billericay Essex............16 E7
Billingborough Lincs...31 G6
Billingham S on T............38 E2
Billinghay Lincs............31 H4
Billingshurst W Susx...9 K3
Bilsby Lincs............31 K3
Bilsthorpe Notts............30 C4
Binbrook Lincs............35 H7
Binfield Br For............14 F6
Bingham Notts............30 D5
Bingley C Brad............33 K3
Birdlip Gloucs............22 A8
Birkenhead Wirral............32 C7
Birmingham Birm............22 B2
Birstall Leics............30 C8
Birtley Gatesd............43 K6
Bishop Auckland Dur...38 C1
Bishop's Castle
Shrops............21 G2
Bishop's Cleeve
Gloucs............22 A7
Bishop's Frome
Herefs............21 K5
Bishops Lydeard
Somset............12 C7
Bishop's Stortford
Herts............16 D5
Bishopsteignton
Devon............6 C4
Bishopston Swans............19 J7
Bishopstone Swindn...13 M3
Bishop Sutton BaNES...13 G5
Bishop's Waltham
Hants............8 F4
Bitchfield Lincs............30 F6
Bitton S Glos............13 G4
Blaby Leics............22 F1
Blackbrook Staffs............28 E6
Blackburn Bl w D............32 F4
Blackford P & K............50 E6
Blackmill Brdgnd............19 M7
Blackpool Bpool............32 C3
Black Torrington
Devon............4 F4
Blackwater IoW............8 F6
Blackwaterfoot
N Ayrs............44 C5
Blackwood Caerph...12 C2
Blackwood S Lans............45 L4
Bladon Oxon............14 C3
Blaenau Ffestiniog
Gwynd............26 F5
Blaenavon Torfn............12 D1
Blaengarw Brdgnd............19 L6
Blaenporth Cerdgn...18 F2
Blagdon N Som............12 F5
Blair Atholl P & K............54 C7
Blairgowrie P & K............51 G2
Blairmore Ag & B............49 K5
Blakeney Gloucs............13 G1
Blakesley Nhants............23 G5
Blanchland Nthumb...43 G6
Blandford Forum
Dorset............7 L2
Blanefield Stirlg............50 B8
Blaxton Donc............34 D6
Blaydon Gatesd............43 J5
Bleadney Somset............12 F6
Bleadon N Som............12 E5
Blean Kent............11 J3
Bleddfa Powys............20 F4

Bletchingley Surrey......10 B3
Bletchley M Keyn............23 J6
Bletsoe Bed............23 K4
Blewbury Oxon............14 C5
Blickling Norfk............25 J3
Blidworth Notts............30 C4
Blindley Heath
Surrey............10 C4
Blisland Cnwll............3 G4
Bloxham Oxon............22 E6
Blubberhouses
N York............38 B7
Blue Anchor Somset......5 J3
Blyth Nthumb............43 K4
Blyton Lincs............34 E7
Boat of Garten
Highld............54 D3
Boddam Abers............61 H5
Bodfari Denbgs............27 J3
Bodfuan Gwynd............26 C6
Bodiam E Susx............10 F5
Bodmin Cnwll............3 G4
Bognor Regis W Susx...9 J6
Bolney W Susx............10 B6
Bolsover Derbys............29 L3
Bolton Bolton............32 F6
Bolton Abbey N York...33 J2
Bolton le Sands
Lancs............37 H6
Bolventor Cnwll............3 H3
Bonar Bridge Highld...64 C8
Bonchester Bridge
Border............42 D1
Bo'ness Falk............46 A2
Bonnyrigg Mdloth............46 D4
Bontnewydd Gwynd...26 D4
Bonvilston V Glam............12 B4
Boot Cumb............36 E3
Bootle Cumb............36 E4
Bootle Sefton............32 C7
Bordeaux Guern............6 b1
Boreham Street
E Susx............10 E6
Borehamwood Herts...15 J4
Boroughbridge
N York............38 D6
Borough Green Kent...10 E3
Borrowash Derbys............29 L6
Borth Cerdgn............20 A2
Borth-y-Gest Gwynd...26 E6
Boscastle Cnwll............3 G2
Bosham W Susx............9 H5
Bosherston Pembks...18 D6
Boston Lincs............31 J5
Boston Spa Leeds............34 B3
Botesdale Suffk............25 H7
Bothel Cumb............41 M7
Bottesford Leics............30 E6
Bough Beech Kent............10 D4
Boughton Street
Kent............11 H3
Boulmer Nthumb............47 M7
Bourne Lincs............31 G7
Bournemouth
Bmouth............8 B6
Bourton Shrops............21 K2
Bourton-on-the-
Water Gloucs............22 C7
Bovey Tracey Devon......6 B4
Bowes Dur............37 M3
Bowmore Ag & B............48 C7
Bowness-on-Solway
Cumb............41 M5
Box Wilts............13 J4
Boxford Suffk............17 H4
Bozeat Nhants............23 J4
Bracadale Highld............56 D5
Brackley Nhants............23 G6
Bracknell Br For............14 F6
Bradford C Brad............33 K4
Bradford-on-Avon
Wilts............13 J5
Brading IoW............8 F6
Bradwell Derbys............29 J2
Bradwell-on-Sea
Essex............17 H6
Bradworthy Devon............4 C6
Brae Shet............61 b4
Braemar Abers............54 E5
Braeswick Ork............65 d2
Braidwood S Lans............45 L3
Brailsford Derbys............29 J5
Braintree Essex............16 F5
Braithwaite Cumb............41 K6
Bramdean Hants............8 F3
Bramfield Suffk............25 K7
Bramham Leeds............34 B3
Bramhope Leeds............33 L3
Bramley Hants............14 D7
Bramley Surrey............9 K2

Brampton Cambs............23 M3
Brampton Cumb............42 D5
Bramshaw Hants............8 D4
Brancaster Norfk............24 E2
Brandesburton
E R Yk............35 H3
Brandon Dur............43 J7
Brandon Suffk............24 E6
Brandon Warwks............22 E3
Branscombe Devon......6 E3
Bransgore Hants............8 C6
Branston Lincs............30 F3
Branthwaite Cumb............36 D2
Brassington Derbys......29 J4
Brasted Kent............10 D3
Bratton Wilts............13 J6
Bratton Clovelly
Devon............3 K2
Bratton Fleming
Devon............4 F4
Braughing Herts............16 C5
Braunton Devon............4 E4
Brayford Devon............4 F4
Breascleit W Isls............62 g3
Breasclete W Isls............62 g3
Brechfa Carmth............19 H4
Brechin Angus............55 J7
Brecon Powys............20 E7
Brede E Susx............11 G6
Bredenbury Herefs......21 K5
Bredhurst Kent............10 F3
Bredon Worcs............22 A6
Bredwardine Herefs......21 G6
Brendon Devon............5 G3
Brent Knoll Somset......12 E6
Brentwood Essex............16 E7
Brenzett Kent............11 H5
Brereton Green
Ches E............28 E4
Brewood Staffs............28 F8
Bride IoM............36 c1
Bridestowe Devon............3 L2
Bridge Kent............11 J3
Bridgend Ag & B............44 C4
Bridgend Ag & B............48 C6
Bridgend Brdgnd............19 L7
Bridge of Allan Stirlg...50 D6
Bridge of Cally P & K...51 G2
Bridge of Earn P & K...51 G5
Bridge of Orchy
Ag & B............53 K6
Bridge of Weir Rens...49 M6
Bridgnorth Shrops............21 L2
Bridgwater Somset............12 D7
Bridlington E R Yk............39 L6
Bridport Dorset............7 H3
Brierfield Lancs............33 H3
Brigg N Linc............35 G6
Brigham Cumb............41 L8
Brighouse Calder............33 K4
Brighstone IoW............8 E7
Brightlingsea Essex......17 J5
Brighton Br & H............10 B7
Brigstock Nhants............23 K2
Brinklow Warwks............22 E3
Brinkworth Wilts............13 K3
Brinyan Ork............65 c3
Bristol Bristl............13 G4
Brixham Torbay............6 C6
Brixton Devon............3 L5
Brixton Gt Lon............15 K6
Brixworth Nhants............23 H3
Broad Blunsdon
Swindn............13 L3
Broad Chalke Wilts......13 K8
Broadclyst Devon............6 D3
Broadford Highld............56 F6
Broad Haven Pembks...18 C5
Broadstairs Kent............11 L2
Broadway Worcs............22 C6
Broadwindsor
Dorset............7 G2
Brockdish Norfk............25 J7
Brockenhurst Hants......8 D5
Brockford Street
Suffk............17 J1
Brockworth Gloucs......21 M8
Brodick N Ayrs............44 D4
Brome Suffk............25 H7
Bromfield Shrops............21 J3
Bromham Bed............23 K5
Bromley Gt Lon............10 C2
Brompton-by-
Sawdon N York............39 J5
Brompton Regis
Somset............5 H4
Bromsgrove Worcs......22 A3
Bromyard Herefs............21 K5
Bronllys Powys............20 F6
Brooke Norfk............25 K6
Brookland Kent............11 H5

Brookmans Park
Herts............15 J4
Broomhill Nthumb............43 K2
Brora Highld............64 F7
Broseley Shrops............21 K1
Brotherton N York............34 B4
Brotton R & Cl............39 G2
Brough Cumb............37 K2
Broughton Border............46 B6
Broughton N Linc............34 F6
Broughton-in-
Furness Cumb............36 F5
Broughton Poggs
Oxon............13 M2
Brownhills Wsall............29 H8
Broxburn W Loth............46 B3
Broxted Essex............16 D5
Brundall Norfk............25 K5
Bruton Somset............13 G6
Brynamman Carmth......19 K5
Bryncrug Gwynd............20 A1
Brynmawr Blae G............12 C1
Bubwith E R Yk............34 E3
Buchlyvie Stirlg............50 B7
Buckden Cambs............23 M4
Buckden N York............37 M5
Buckfastleigh Devon......6 B5
Buckhaven Fife............51 H6
Buckhorn Weston
Dorset............13 H8
Buckie Moray............60 B3
Buckingham Bucks............23 G6
Buckland Herts............16 C4
Bucklers Hard Hants......8 D6
Buckley Flints............27 L4
Bucklow Hill Ches E......28 E2
Buckminster Leics............30 E7
Bude Cnwll............4 B6
Budleigh Salterton
Devon............6 D4
Bugle Cnwll............2 F5
Builth Wells Powys......20 E5
Bulford Wilts............8 C2
Bulkington Warwks......22 E2
Bulphan Thurr............16 E8
Bulwick Nhants............23 K2
Bunessan Ag & B............48 C2
Bungay Suffk............25 K6
Bunny Notts............30 C6
Buntingford Herts............16 C4
Bunwell Norfk............25 H6
Burbage Wilts............13 M5
Bures Essex............17 G4
Burford Oxon............13 M1
Burgess Hill W Susx...10 B6
Burgh by Sands
Cumb............42 B6
Burgh Castle Norfk......25 L5
Burghead Moray............59 J3
Burghfield W Berk............14 D6
Burgh le Marsh Lincs...31 K4
Burley Hants............8 C5
Burleydam Ches E............28 D5
Burley in
Wharfedale
C Brad............33 K3
Burlton Shrops............28 C7
Burneston N York............38 C5
Burnham Market
Norfk............24 F2
Burnham-on-Crouch
Essex............17 H7
Burnham-on-Sea
Somset............12 D6
Burnham Overy
Staithe Norfk............24 F2
Burnley Lancs............33 G4
Burnopfield Dur............43 J6
Burntisland Fife............46 C2
Burravoe Shet............61 d3
Burrelton P & K............51 G3
Burrington Devon............4 F5
Burry Port Carmth............19 H6
Burscough Bridge
Lancs............32 D5
Bursledon Hants............8 E5
Burton Ches W............27 L3
Burton Agnes E R Yk...39 K6
Burton Bradstock
Dorset............7 H3
Burton Fleming
E R Yk............39 K6
Burton-in-Kendal
Cumb............37 H5
Burton Joyce Notts......30 C5
Burton Latimer
Nhants............23 J3
Burton upon
Stather N Linc............34 F5
Burton upon Trent
Staffs............29 J7

Burwash E Susx....10 E5
Burwell Cambs....16 E1
Burwick Ork....65 c6
Bury Bury....33 G5
Bury St Edmunds
 Suffk....17 G2
Bushey Herts....15 H4
Butley Suffk....17 L3
Buttermere Cumb....36 E2
Butterwick Lincs....31 J5
Buttington Powys....27 K8
Buxted E Susx....10 D6
Buxton Derbys....29 H3
Bwlch Powys....20 F7
Byfleet Surrey....15 H7
Bylchau Conwy....27 H4
Byrness Nthumb....42 F2

C

Cadgwith Cnwll....2 D8
Caerleon Newpt....12 E3
Caernarfon Gwynd....26 D4
Caerphilly Caerph....12 C3
Caersws Powys....20 E2
Caerwent Mons....12 F3
Caerwys Flints....27 J3
Cairndow Ag & B....49 K3
Cairnryan D & G....40 B5
Caister-on-Sea Norfk....25 L5
Caistor Lincs....35 H6
Caldbeck Cumb....42 B7
Caldecott Rutlnd....23 J2
Calder Bridge Cumb....36 D3
Caldercruix N Lans....45 L2
Caldicot Mons....12 F3
Calfsound Ork....65 d2
Calgary Ag & B....52 B5
Callander Stirlg....50 B6
Callington Cnwll....3 J4
Calne Wilts....13 K4
Calshot Hants....8 E5
Calvine P & K....54 C7
Camber E Susx....11 H6
Camberley Surrey....14 F7
Cambo Nthumb....43 H4
Camborne Cnwll....2 C6
Cambourne Cambs....16 B2
Cambridge Cambs....16 C2
Cambridge Gloucs....13 H2
Cambuslang S Lans....45 K2
Camden Town Gt Lon....15 K5
Camelford Cnwll....3 G3
Campbeltown Ag & B....44 B5
Candlesby Lincs....31 K3
Cannich Highld....58 C6
Cannington Somset....12 D7
Cannock Staffs....29 G8
Canonbie D & G....42 C4
Canterbury Kent....11 J3
Canvey Island Essex....16 F8
Caoles Ag & B....48 b2
Capel Surrey....9 L2
Capel Bangor Cerdgn....20 B3
Capel Curig Conwy....26 F4
Capel St Mary Suffk....17 J4
Caputh P & K....50 F3
Carbost Highld....56 D6
Cardiff Cardif....12 C4
Cardigan Cerdgn....18 E2
Cardington Bed....23 L5
Cardross Ag & B....49 L5
Carew Pembks....18 D6
Carfraemill Border....46 F4
Carhampton Somset....5 J3
Cark Cumb....37 G5
Carlabhagh W Isls....62 g3
Carlisle Cumb....42 C6
Carlops Border....46 C4
Carloway W Isls....62 g3
Carlton N York....34 D4
Carlton N York....38 A5
Carlton-on-Trent
 Notts....30 E4
Carluke S Lans....45 L3
Carmarthen Carmth....19 G4
Carnaby E R Yk....39 K6
Carnforth Lancs....37 H6
Carno Powys....20 D2
Carnon Downs Cnwll....2 E6
Carnoustie Angus....51 K4
Carnwath S Lans....46 A5
Carradale Ag & B....44 C4
Carrbridge Highld....59 H6
Carrefour Jersey....7 b1
Carrick Castle Ag & B....49 K4
Carronbridge D & G....41 J3
Carrutherstown
 D & G....41 L5

Carsphairn D & G....40 F3
Carstairs S Lans....45 M3
Carterton Oxon....14 A3
Cartmel Cumb....37 G5
Castel Guern....6 a2
Casterton Cumb....37 J5
Castle Acre Norfk....24 F4
Castlebay W Isls....62 b14
Castle Carrock Cumb....42 D6
Castle Cary Somset....13 G7
Castle Donington
 Leics....29 L6
Castle Douglas D & G....41 H5
Castleford Wakefd....34 B4
Castle Hedingham
 Essex....16 F4
Castlemartin Pembks....18 C6
Castle Rising Norfk....24 D4
Castleside Dur....43 H6
Castleton Derbys....29 H2
Castleton N York....39 G3
Castleton Newpt....12 D3
Castletown Highld....65 H2
Castletown IoM....36 b4
Caterham Surrey....10 C3
Catfield Norfk....25 K4
Caton Lancs....37 H6
Catrine E Ayrs....45 J5
Catsfield E Susx....10 F6
Catterick N York....38 C4
Caunton Notts....30 D4
Cawdor Highld....59 G4
Cawsand Cnwll....3 K5
Caxton Cambs....16 B2
Caythorpe Lincs....30 F5
Cayton N York....39 K5
Cemaes IoA....26 C1
Cemmaes Road
 Powys....20 C1
Ceres Fife....51 J5
Cerne Abbas Dorset....7 J2
Cerrigydrudion
 Conwy....27 H5
Chadderton Oldham....33 H6
Chadlington Oxon....14 B2
Chagford Devon....6 A3
Chale IoW....8 E7
Chalfont St Giles
 Bucks....15 G4
Chalfont St Peter
 Bucks....15 G5
Chalford Gloucs....13 J2
Challacombe Devon....4 F3
Challock Kent....11 H3
Chandler's Ford
 Hants....8 E4
Chapel-en-le-Frith
 Derbys....29 H2
Chapel St Leonards
 Lincs....31 L3
Chapeltown Sheff....34 A6
Chapmanslade Wilts....13 J6
Chard Somset....6 F2
Charing Kent....11 H4
Charlbury Oxon....14 B2
Charlecote Warwks....22 D5
Charlton Kings
 Gloucs....22 A7
Charlton Marshall
 Dorset....7 L2
Charlwood Surrey....10 B4
Charmouth Dorset....7 G2
Chartham Kent....11 J3
Chatburn Lancs....33 G3
Chatham Medway....10 F2
Chatteris Cambs....24 B7
Chatton Nthumb....47 K6
Chawleigh Devon....4 H4
Chawton Hants....9 G3
Cheadle Staffs....29 G5
Cheadle Stockp....33 H7
Cheddar Somset....12 F6
Cheddleton Staffs....29 G5
Chelford Ches E....28 F2
Chelmsford Essex....16 F6
Cheltenham Gloucs....22 A7
Chepstow Mons....12 F3
Cheriton Hants....8 F3
Cheriton Fitzpaine
 Devon....5 H6
Chertsey Surrey....15 G6
Chesham Bucks....15 G4
Cheshunt Herts....15 K4
Chester Ches W....28 D3
Chesterfield Derbys....29 K3
Chester-le-Street Dur....43 K5
Chew Magna BaNES....13 G5
Chewton Mendip
 Somset....13 G6
Chicheley M Keyn....23 J5
Chichester W Susx....9 H5

Chickerell Dorset....7 J4
Chicklade Wilts....13 J7
Chiddingfold Surrey....9 J3
Chieveley W Berk....14 C6
Chigwell Essex....16 C7
Childer Thornton
 Ches W....28 B3
Chilham Kent....11 J3
Chillington Devon....6 B7
Chilmark Wilts....13 K7
Chilsworthy Devon....4 C6
Chilton Foliat Wilts....14 A6
Chineham Hants....14 D7
Chinnor Oxon....14 E4
Chippenham Cambs....16 E1
Chippenham Wilts....13 J4
Chipperfield Herts....15 G4
Chipping Lancs....32 F3
Chipping Campden
 Gloucs....22 C6
Chipping Norton
 Oxon....22 D7
Chipping Ongar
 Essex....16 D6
Chipping Sodbury
 S Glos....13 H3
Chipping Warden
 Nhants....22 F5
Chirbury Shrops....21 G1
Chirk Wrexhm....27 L6
Chirnside Border....47 J4
Chiseldon Swindn....13 M4
Chitterne Wilts....13 K6
Chittlehamholt
 Devon....4 F5
Chobham Surrey....15 G7
Cholderton Wilts....8 C2
Chorley Lancs....32 E5
Chorleywood Herts....15 G4
Christchurch Dorset....8 C6
Chudleigh Devon....6 C4
Chudleigh Knighton
 Devon....6 C4
Chulmleigh Devon....4 F6
Churchill Oxon....14 A2
Churchstoke Powys....21 G2
Church Stretton
 Shrops....21 H2
Churston Ferrers
 Torbay....6 C6
Churt Surrey....9 H3
Cinderford Gloucs....21 K8
Cirencester Gloucs....13 K2
Clachan Ag & B....44 B3
Clachan Highld....56 E5
Clackmannan Clacks....50 E7
Clacton-on-Sea Essex....17 J5
Clanfield Oxon....14 A4
Claonaig Ag & B....44 C3
Clapham Bed....23 K5
Clapham N York....37 K6
Clare Suffk....16 F3
Clatt Abers....60 C6
Claverdon Warwks....22 C4
Clavering Essex....16 D4
Clawton Devon....4 C7
Clay Cross Derbys....29 K4
Claydon Suffk....17 J3
Cleator Moor Cumb....36 D2
Cleethorpes NE Lin....35 J6
Cleeve N Som....12 F5
Cleeve Hill Gloucs....22 B7
Cleobury Mortimer
 Shrops....21 K3
Cleobury North
 Shrops....21 K2
Clevedon N Som....12 E4
Cleveleys Lancs....32 C3
Cley next the Sea
 Norfk....25 G2
Cliffe Medway....10 F2
Cliffe N York....34 D4
Cliffe Woods Medway....10 F2
Clifton Cumb....37 H2
Clifton upon Teme
 Worcs....21 L4
Climping W Susx....9 K5
Clitheroe Lancs....33 G3
Clola Abers....61 G5
Clophill C Beds....23 L6
Closworth Somset....7 H2
Cloughton N York....39 J4
Clova Angus....55 G6
Clovelly Devon....4 C5
Clovenfords Border....46 E6
Clowne Derbys....30 B3
Clows Top Worcs....21 L3
Clun Shrops....21 G3
Clydach Swans....19 J6
Clydebank W Duns....45 H2
Clynder Ag & B....49 K5

Clynnog-fawr Gwynd....26 D5
Clyro Powys....20 F6
Clyst St Mary Devon....6 D3
Coalport Wrekin....21 K1
Coalville Leics....29 L7
Coatbridge N Lans....45 K2
Cobham Kent....10 E2
Cockburnspath
 Border....47 H3
Cockermouth Cumb....41 L8
Cocking W Susx....9 J4
Coddenham Suffk....17 J2
Codford St Mary
 Wilts....13 K7
Codicote Herts....15 J3
Codnor Derbys....29 L5
Codsall Staffs....21 M1
Coedpoeth Wrexhm....27 L5
Coggeshall Essex....17 G5
Colchester Essex....17 H5
Cold Ash W Berk....14 C6
Cold Ashby Nhants....23 G3
Cold Ashton S Glos....13 H4
Coldingham Border....47 J4
Cold Norton Essex....17 G7
Coldstream Border....47 H5
Coleford Gloucs....13 G1
Colerne Wilts....13 J4
Coleshill Warwks....22 C2
Colintraive Ag & B....49 J6
Collier's End Herts....15 K2
Collieston Abers....61 G6
Collingbourne Ducis
 Wilts....13 M6
Collingham Leeds....34 B3
Colmonell S Ayrs....40 C3
Colne Lancs....33 H3
Colne Engaine Essex....17 G4
Coln St Aldwyns
 Gloucs....13 L2
Colpy Abers....60 D6
Colsterworth Lincs....30 F7
Coltishall Norfk....25 J4
Colwell Nthumb....43 G4
Colwyn Bay Conwy....27 G2
Colyford Devon....6 F3
Colyton Devon....6 F3
Combe Martin Devon....4 E3
Compton Surrey....9 J2
Compton W Berk....14 C5
Comrie P & K....50 D5
Congleton Ches E....28 F4
Congresbury N Som....12 E5
Coningsby Lincs....31 H4
Conington Cambs....23 M2
Conisbrough Donc....34 C6
Coniston Cumb....36 F3
Connah's Quay Flints....28 C3
Connel Ag & B....52 F7
Conon Bridge Highld....58 E4
Consett Dur....43 H6
Constantine Cnwll....2 D7
Contin Highld....58 D4
Conwy Conwy....27 G3
Cookham W & M....14 F5
Coolham W Susx....9 L4
Coombe Bissett Wilts....8 B3
Coombe Hill Gloucs....21 M7
Copdock Suffk....17 J3
Copford Green Essex....17 G5
Copley Dur....38 B2
Copplestone Devon....5 G6
Copthorne W Susx....10 B4
Corbiere Jersey....7 a2
Corbridge Nthumb....43 G5
Corby Nhants....23 J2
Corby Glen Lincs....30 F7
Corfe Somset....6 F1
Corfe Castle Dorset....7 M4
Corgarff Abers....55 G4
Cornhill-on-Tweed
 Nthumb....47 H5
Cornwood Devon....3 L5
Corpach Highld....53 H3
Corrie N Ayrs....44 D4
Corris Gwynd....26 F8
Corsham Wilts....13 J4
Corston Wilts....13 J3
Corton Suffk....25 M6
Cosby Leics....22 F2
Cotebrook Ches W....28 D4
Cotherstone Dur....38 A2
Cottenham Cambs....16 C1
Cottered Herts....16 B4
Cottingham E R Yk....35 G4
Coulport Ag & B....49 K5
Coulter S Lans....46 B6
Countesthorpe Leics....23 G2
Coupar Angus P & K....51 G3

Cove Highld ... 62 D8
Coventry Covtry ... 22 E3
Coverack Cnwll ... 2 D8
Cowbit Lincs ... 31 H7
Cowbridge V Glam ... 12 B4
Cowden Kent ... 10 D4
Cowdenbeath Fife ... 51 G7
Cowes IoW ... 8 E6
Cowfold W Susx ... 9 L4
Cowling N York ... 33 J3
Coxheath Kent ... 10 F3
Coxwold N York ... 38 E5
Coylton S Ayrs ... 45 H6
Coylumbridge Highld ... 54 D3
Crackington Haven
Cnwll ... 4 B7
Cracoe N York ... 37 M7
Crafthole Cnwll ... 3 J5
Craigellachie Moray ... 59 L5
Craighouse Ag & B ... 48 D6
Craignure Ag & B ... 52 E6
Craigrothie Fife ... 51 J5
Crail Fife ... 51 L6
Crailing Border ... 47 G7
Cramlington Nthumb ... 43 K4
Cranborne Dorset ... 8 B4
Cranbrook Kent ... 10 F5
Cranfield C Beds ... 23 K6
Cranham Gloucs ... 21 M8
Cranleigh Surrey ... 9 K2
Cranshaws Border ... 47 G4
Crarae Ag & B ... 49 H4
Craster Nthumb ... 47 M7
Crathie Abers ... 54 F5
Crathorne N York ... 38 E3
Craven Arms Shrops ... 21 H3
Crawford S Lans ... 46 A7
Crawfordjohn S Lans ... 45 M5
Crawley W Susx ... 10 B5
Crawley Down
W Susx ... 10 B4
Creag Ghoraidh
W Isls ... 62 c10
Creagorry W Isls ... 62 c10
Credenhill Herefs ... 21 H6
Crediton Devon ... 5 G7
Creetown D & G ... 40 F6
Cregneash IoM ... 36 a4
Cressage Shrops ... 21 K1
Crewe Ches E ... 28 E4
Crewkerne Somset ... 7 G2
Crianlarich Stirlg ... 53 K7
Criccieth Gwynd ... 26 D6
Crickhowell Powys ... 20 F7
Cricklade Wilts ... 13 L3
Crieff P & K ... 50 D5
Crimond Abers ... 61 H4
Crinan Ag & B ... 49 G4
Cringleford Norfk ... 25 J5
Crockernwell Devon ... 6 B3
Crocketford D & G ... 41 J4
Croglin Cumb ... 42 D6
Cromarty Highld ... 59 G3
Cromdale Highld ... 59 J6
Cromer Norfk ... 25 J2
Cromford Derbys ... 29 K4
Cromwell Notts ... 30 E4
Crook Dur ... 43 J7
Crooklands Cumb ... 37 H5
Cropredy Oxon ... 22 F5
Cropton N York ... 39 G4
Crosby IoM ... 36 b3
Crosby Sefton ... 32 C6
Crossford Fife ... 46 B2
Crossford S Lans ... 45 L3
Cross Hands Carmth ... 19 H5
Crosshill S Ayrs ... 45 G6
Cross in Hand E Susx ... 10 D6
Crosskeys Caerph ... 12 D3
Crossmichael D & G ... 41 H5
Crossway Green
Worcs ... 21 M4
Crosthwaite Cumb ... 37 G4
Crowborough E Susx ... 10 D5
Crowcombe Somset ... 5 K4
Crowhurst E Susx ... 10 F6
Crowland Lincs ... 31 H8
Crowle N Linc ... 34 D6
Crowthorne Wokham ... 14 H7
Croxton Kerrial Leics ... 30 E6
Croy Highld ... 59 G4
Croyde Devon ... 4 D4
Croydon Gt Lon ... 15 K7
Cruden Bay Abers ... 61 H4
Crudgington Wrekin ... 28 D7
Crudwell Wilts ... 13 K3
Crynant Neath ... 19 K5
Cuckfield W Susx ... 10 B5
Cuckney Notts ... 30 C3
Cuddington Ches W ... 28 D3
Cudworth Barns ... 34 B6

Cuffley Herts ... 15 K4
Culgaith Cumb ... 37 J1
Cullen Moray ... 60 C3
Cullompton Devon ... 5 J6
Culmstock Devon ... 5 K6
Cumbernauld N Lans ... 45 L1
Cuminestown Abers ... 60 E4
Cummertrees D & G ... 41 L5
Cumnock E Ayrs ... 45 J5
Cumnor Oxon ... 14 C4
Cumrew Cumb ... 42 D6
Cupar Fife ... 51 J5
Curry Rivel Somset ... 12 E8
Cwmbran Torfn ... 12 D2
Cwmystwyth Cerdgn ... 20 C3
Cymer Neath ... 19 L6
Cynwyl Elfed Carmth ... 19 G4

D

Dailly S Ayrs ... 40 D2
Dairsie Fife ... 51 J5
Dalbeattie D & G ... 41 J5
Dalby IoM ... 36 a3
Dale Pembks ... 18 B5
Dalgety Bay Fife ... 46 C2
Dalhalvaig Highld ... 64 E3
Dalkeith Mdloth ... 46 D3
Dallas Moray ... 59 J4
Dalmally Ag & B ... 53 J7
Dalmellington E Ayrs ... 45 H7
Dalry N Ayrs ... 45 G3
Dalrymple E Ayrs ... 45 G6
Dalston Cumb ... 42 B6
Dalton D & G ... 41 L4
Dalton-in-Furness
Cumb ... 36 F6
Dalwhinnie Highld ... 54 A3
Damerham Hants ... 8 B4
Danbury Essex ... 16 F6
Darlington Darltn ... 38 C2
Darras Hall Nthumb ... 43 J5
Darrington Wakefd ... 34 B5
Dartford Kent ... 10 D2
Dartington Devon ... 6 B5
Dartmouth Devon ... 6 C6
Darvel E Ayrs ... 45 J4
Darwen Bl w D ... 32 F5
Datchet W & M ... 15 G6
Dava Highld ... 59 H5
Davenham Ches W ... 28 D3
Daventry Nhants ... 23 G4
Daviot Highld ... 58 F5
Dawlish Devon ... 6 C4
Deal Kent ... 11 L3
Dearham Cumb ... 41 L7
Debenham Suffk ... 17 J2
Deddington Oxon ... 22 F6
Dedham Essex ... 17 H4
Deeping St James
Lincs ... 31 H8
Deeping St Nicholas
Lincs ... 31 H7
Deganwy Conwy ... 27 G2
Delabole Cnwll ... 3 G3
Denbigh Denbgs ... 27 J3
Denby Dale Kirk ... 33 L6
Denham Bucks ... 15 G5
Denholm Border ... 9 G5
Denmead Hants ... 9 F7
Dennington Suffk ... 17 K1
Denny Falk ... 50 D8
Densole Kent ... 11 K4
Dent Cumb ... 37 K5
Denton Tamesd ... 33 H7
Derby C Derb ... 29 K6
Dereham Norfk ... 24 E5
Dersingham Norfk ... 24 E3
Dervaig Ag & B ... 52 B5
Desborough Nhants ... 23 H3
Desford Leics ... 22 F1
Devil's Bridge Cerdgn ... 20 B3
Devizes Wilts ... 13 K5
Dewsbury Kirk ... 33 L5
Dial Post W Susx ... 9 L4
Didcot Oxon ... 14 C5
Didmarton Gloucs ... 13 J3
Digby Lincs ... 31 G4
Dilwyn Herefs ... 21 H5
Dinas-Mawddwy
Gwynd ... 27 G7
Dingwall Highld ... 58 E4
Dinnington Rothm ... 30 B2
Dippen Ag & B ... 44 C4
Diseworth Leics ... 29 L7
Dishforth N York ... 38 D6
Disley Ches E ... 29 G2
Diss Norfk ... 25 H7

Ditchling E Susx ... 10 B6
Dittisham Devon ... 6 C6
Ditton Priors Shrops ... 21 K2
Dobwalls Cnwll ... 3 H4
Docking Norfk ... 24 E3
Doddington Cambs ... 24 B6
Doddington Kent ... 11 G3
Doddington Nthumb ... 47 K6
Dodworth Barns ... 33 L6
Dolgellau Gwynd ... 26 F7
Dollar Clacks ... 50 E6
Dolphinton S Lans ... 46 B3
Dolton Devon ... 4 E6
Dolwyddelan Conwy ... 26 F5
Doncaster Donc ... 34 C6
Donington Lincs ... 31 H6
Dorchester Dorset ... 7 K3
Dorchester Oxon ... 14 D4
Dordon Warwks ... 22 D1
Dores Highld ... 58 E5
Dorking Surrey ... 9 L2
Dornie Highld ... 57 H6
Dornoch Highld ... 59 G1
Dorrington Shrops ... 21 J1
Dorstone Herefs ... 21 G6
Douglas IoM ... 36 c3
Douglas S Lans ... 45 L5
Dounby Ork ... 65 b3
Doune Stirlg ... 50 C6
Dousland Devon ... 3 L4
Dover Kent ... 11 L4
Doveridge Derbys ... 29 H6
Dowally P & K ... 50 E3
Downderry Cnwll ... 3 J5
Downham Market
Norfk ... 24 D5
Downton Wilts ... 8 C4
Drakes Broughton
Worcs ... 22 A5
Draycott Somset ... 12 F6
Drayton Norfk ... 25 J4
Drayton Oxon ... 14 C4
Driffield E R Yk ... 39 J7
Drimnin Highld ... 52 C5
Droitwich Worcs ... 22 A4
Dronfield Derbys ... 29 K3
Droxford Hants ... 8 F4
Drumbeg Highld ... 63 G4
Drummore D & G ... 40 C7
Drumnadrochit
Highld ... 58 D6
Drymen Stirlg ... 50 A7
Drynoch Highld ... 56 D6
Duddington Nhants ... 23 K1
Dudley Dudley ... 22 A2
Duffield Derbys ... 29 K5
Dufftown Moray ... 59 L5
Duffus Moray ... 59 K3
Dulnain Bridge Highld ... 59 H6
Dulverton Somset ... 5 H4
Dumbarton W Duns ... 49 M5
Dumfries D & G ... 41 K4
Dunbar E Loth ... 47 G2
Dunbeath Highld ... 65 H5
Dunblane Stirlg ... 50 D6
Dunchurch Warwks ... 22 F3
Dundee C Dund ... 51 J4
Dundonald S Ayrs ... 45 G4
Dundonnell Highld ... 57 K1
Dundrennan D & G ... 41 H6
Dunfermline Fife ... 46 B2
Dunkeld P & K ... 50 F3
Dunlop E Ayrs ... 45 H3
Dunnet Highld ... 65 H2
Dunning P & K ... 50 F5
Dunoon Ag & B ... 49 K5
Dunragit D & G ... 40 C6
Duns Border ... 47 H4
Dunscore D & G ... 41 J4
Dunsfold Surrey ... 9 K3
Dunsford Devon ... 6 B3
Dunsop Bridge Lancs ... 32 F2
Dunstable C Beds ... 15 G2
Dunster Somset ... 5 J3
Duntish Dorset ... 7 K3
Dunure S Ayrs ... 44 F6
Dunvant Swans ... 19 J6
Dunvegan Highld ... 56 C4
Dunwich Suffk ... 25 L8
Durham Dur ... 43 K7
Durness Highld ... 63 J2
Duror Highld ... 53 G5
Durrington Wilts ... 8 C2
Durris Abers ... 55 L5
Dursley Gloucs ... 13 H2
Duxford Cambs ... 16 D3
Dyce C Aber ... 55 M3
Dyffryn Ardudwy
Gwynd ... 26 E7
Dymchurch Kent ... 11 J5
Dymock Gloucs ... 21 K7

E

Eaglesfield D & G ... 42 A4
Eaglesham E Rens ... 45 J3
Ealing Gt Lon ... 15 J5
Earby Lancs ... 33 H3
Eardisley Herefs ... 21 G5
Earith Cambs ... 24 B7
Earley Wokham ... 14 E6
Earls Barton Nhants ... 23 J4
Earls Colne Essex ... 17 G4
Earl Shilton Leics ... 22 F1
Earlston Border ... 46 F6
Earsham Norfk ... 25 K6
Easdale Ag & B ... 48 F2
Easebourne W Susx ... 9 J4
Easington Dur ... 43 L7
Easington E R Yk ... 35 K5
Easingwold N York ... 38 E6
East Ayton N York ... 39 J5
East Barkwith Lincs ... 31 H2
East Bergholt Suffk ... 17 J4
Eastbourne E Susx ... 10 D8
East Chinnock
Somset ... 7 H1
Eastchurch Kent ... 11 H2
East Cowes IoW ... 8 E6
East Dean E Susx ... 10 D8
East Dean W Susx ... 9 J4
East Goscote Leics ... 30 C7
East Grinstead
W Susx ... 10 C4
East Harling Norfk ... 25 G6
East Hoathly E Susx ... 10 D6
East Horsley Surrey ... 15 H8
East Ilsley W Berk ... 14 C5
East Kilbride S Lans ... 45 J3
East Knoyle Wilts ... 13 J7
East Lavant W Susx ... 9 H5
Eastleigh Hants ... 8 E4
East Linton E Loth ... 46 F3
East Lulworth Dorset ... 7 L4
Easton Suffk ... 17 K2
East Prawle Devon ... 6 B7
East Preston W Susx ... 9 J5
Eastriggs D & G ... 42 A5
East Rudham Norfk ... 24 F3
Eastry Kent ... 11 L3
East Saltoun E Loth ... 46 E3
East Stoke Notts ... 30 D5
East Wittering
W Susx ... 9 H6
East Witton N York ... 38 B5
Eastwood Notts ... 29 L5
Eaton Socon Cambs ... 23 L4
Ebbw Vale Blae G ... 12 C1
Ebchester Dur ... 43 H6
Ecclefechan D & G ... 41 M4
Eccles Border ... 47 H5
Eccleshall Staffs ... 28 F6
Echt Abers ... 55 K4
Eckington Derbys ... 29 L2
Eckington Worcs ... 22 A6
Edderton Highld ... 58 F2
Eddleston Border ... 46 C5
Edenbridge Kent ... 10 C4
Edinbane Highld ... 56 D4
Edinburgh C Edin ... 46 C3
Edlington Lincs ... 31 H3
Edmundbyers Dur ... 43 H6
Ednam Border ... 47 G6
Edwinstowe Notts ... 30 C3
Edzell Angus ... 55 J7
Effingham Surrey ... 15 H7
Eggesford Devon ... 4 F6
Eggleston Dur ... 37 M2
Egham Surrey ... 15 G6
Eglingham Nthumb ... 47 K7
Eglwyswrw Pembks ... 18 E3
Egremont Cumb ... 36 D3
Egton Bridge N York ... 39 H4
Elan Village Powys ... 20 D4
Elgin Moray ... 59 K3
Elgol Highld ... 56 E7
Elham Kent ... 11 J4
Elie Fife ... 51 K6
Elkesley Notts ... 30 D3
Elkstone Gloucs ... 13 K1
Elland Calder ... 33 K5
Ellesmere Shrops ... 28 B6
Ellesmere Port
Ches W ... 28 B3
Ellingham Norfk ... 25 K6
Ellon Abers ... 61 H6
Elloughton E R Yk ... 34 F4
Elmstead Market
Essex ... 17 H5
Elsdon Nthumb ... 43 G3
Elsrickle S Lans ... 46 B5
Elstead Surrey ... 9 J2

Elstree Herts 15 J4
Elterwater Cumb 37 G3
Eltisley Cambs 16 B2
Elton Cambs 23 L2
Elveden Suffk 24 F7
Elvetham Heath
　Hants 14 E7
Elvington C York 34 D3
Elworthy Somset 5 J4
Ely Cambs 24 C7
Embleton Nthumb 47 M7
Embo Highld 64 E8
Empingham Rutlnd 30 F8
Emsworth Hants 9 H5
Enderby Leics 22 F1
Enfield Gt Lon 15 K4
Ennerdale Bridge
　Cumb 36 D2
Enstone Oxon 14 B4
Epping Essex 16 C6
Epsom Surrey 15 J7
Epworth N Linc 34 E6
Errogie Highld 58 E6
Errol P & K 51 H4
Erwood Powys 20 E6
Esher Surrey 15 H7
Eskdale Green Cumb 36 E4
Eskdalemuir D & G 42 A3
Essendine Rutlnd 31 G8
Essendon Herts 15 J3
Eston R & Cl 38 E2
Etal Nthumb 47 J6
Etchingham E Susx 10 F5
Eton W & M 15 G6
Ettington Warwks 22 B5
Ettrick Border 46 D7
Ettrickbridge Border 46 E7
Evanton Highld 58 E3
Evercreech Somset 13 G7
Eversley Hants 14 E7
Evesham Worcs 22 B6
Ewen Gloucs 13 K2
Ewhurst Surrey 9 K2
Ewyas Harold Herefs 21 H7
Exebridge Somset 5 H5
Exeter Devon 6 C3
Exford Somset 5 H4
Exminster Devon 6 C3
Exmouth Devon 6 D4
Eye C Pete 23 M1
Eye Suffk 25 H7
Eyemouth Border 47 J4
Eynsford Kent 10 D2
Eynsham Oxon 14 B3

F

Failsworth Oldham 33 H6
Fairbourne Gwynd 26 E8
Fairford Gloucs 13 L2
Fairlie N Ayrs 44 F3
Fairlight E Susx 11 G6
Fakenham Norfk 24 F3
Fala Mdloth 46 E4
Faldingworth Lincs 31 G2
Falfield S Glos 13 G3
Falkirk Falk 50 E8
Falkland Fife 51 H6
Falmouth Cnwll 2 E7
Falstone Nthumb 42 E3
Fareham Hants 8 F5
Faringdon Oxon 14 A4
Farnborough Hants 14 F7
Farnell Angus 51 L2
Farnham Surrey 9 H2
Farnham Common
　Bucks 15 G5
Farningham Kent 10 D2
Far Sawrey Cumb 37 G4
Fauldhouse W Loth 45 M2
Faversham Kent 11 H3
Fawley Hants 8 F5
Fazeley Staffs 22 C1
Fearnan P & K 50 C3
Felixstowe Suffk 17 K4
Felsted Essex 16 E5
Felton Nthumb 43 J2
Feltwell Norfk 24 E6
Fenny Bentley
　Derbys 29 J5
Fenny Bridges Devon 6 E3
Fenny Compton
　Warwks 22 E1
Fenny Drayton Leics 22 E1
Fenwick E Ayrs 45 H4
Ferndown Dorset 8 B5
Fernhill Heath Worcs 21 M4
Fernhurst W Susx 9 H3
Fernilee Derbys 29 G3

Ferring W Susx 9 K5
Ferryhill Dur 43 K8
Fettercairn Abers 55 K6
Ffestiniog Gwynd 26 F5
Filby Norfk 25 L4
Filey N York 39 K5
Fincham Norfk 24 E5
Finchingfield Essex 16 E4
Findhorn Moray 59 J3
Findochty Moray 60 C3
Findon W Susx 9 L5
Finedon Nhants 23 J3
Finningham Suffk 17 H1
Finningley Donc 34 D6
Finstown Ork 65 b4
Fintry Stirlg 50 B7
Fionnphort Ag & B 48 C2
Firle E Susx 10 D7
Fishbourne IoW 8 F6
Fishguard Pembks 18 C3
Fittleworth W Susx 9 K4
Fitzhead Somset 5 K4
Five Oaks Jersey 7 c2
Fladdabister Shet 61 c6
Flamborough E R Yk 39 L6
Flamstead Herts 15 H3
Fleet Hants 14 F7
Fleetwood Lancs 32 C3
Flimby Cumb 41 K7
Flint Flints 27 K3
Flitwick C Beds 23 K6
Flixton N York 39 K5
Flore Nhants 23 G4
Fochabers Moray 59 L4
Folkestone Kent 11 K5
Folkingham Lincs 31 G6
Fontmell Magna
　Dorset 7 L1
Fontwell W Susx 9 J5
Ford Nthumb 47 J6
Fordcombe Kent 10 D4
Fordingbridge Hants 8 C4
Fordoun Abers 55 K6
Fordwich Kent 11 J3
Forest Guern 6 a2
Forest Row E Susx 10 C5
Forfar Angus 51 J2
Formby Sefton 32 C6
Forres Moray 59 J4
Fort Augustus Highld 58 C7
Forteviot P & K 50 F5
Forth S Lans 45 M3
Fortingall P & K 50 C3
Forton Lancs 32 E2
Fortrose Highld 58 F4
Fortuneswell Dorset 7 J4
Fort William Highld 53 H4
Foston Lincs 30 E5
Four Crosses Powys 27 L7
Four Marks Hants 9 G3
Fowey Cnwll 3 G5
Fownhope Herefs 21 J6
Foxdale IoM 36 b3
Foyers Highld 58 D7
Framlingham Suffk 17 K2
Frampton Dorset 7 J3
Frant E Susx 10 E5
Fraserburgh Abers 61 G3
Freckenham Suffk 24 D8
Freckleton Lancs 32 D4
Frensham Surrey 9 H2
Freshwater IoW 8 D6
Fressingfield Suffk 25 J7
Freswick Highld 65 J2
Fridaythorpe E R Yk 39 H7
Frilford Oxon 14 B4
Frinton-on-Sea Essex 17 K5
Friockheim Angus 51 K2
Fritton Norfk 25 L5
Frizington Cumb 36 D2
Frocester Gloucs 13 H2
Frodsham Ches W 28 C3
Frome Somset 13 H6
Froxfield Wilts 14 A6
Funtington W Susx 9 H5
Furnace Ag & B 49 J4
Furness Vale Derbys 29 G2
Fyfield Essex 16 D6
Fyfield Oxon 14 B4
Fyvie Abers 60 E5

G

Gailey Staffs 28 F8
Gainford Dur 38 B2
Gainsborough Lincs 34 E7
Gairloch Highld 57 H2
Gairlochy Highld 53 J3
Galashiels Border 46 E6

Galgate Lancs 37 H7
Galston E Ayrs 45 H4
Gamlingay Cambs 16 B3
Gamston Notts 30 D3
Ganllwyd Gwynd 26 F7
Garboldisham Norfk 25 G7
Gardenstown Abers 60 E3
Garelochhead Ag & B 49 K4
Garforth Leeds 34 B4
Gargrave N York 33 H2
Garlieston D & G 40 F6
Garlogie Abers 55 L4
Garrigill Cumb 42 E7
Garstang Lancs 32 E3
Garth Powys 20 D5
Garvald E Loth 46 F3
Garve Highld 58 C3
Gatehouse of Fleet
　D & G 41 G6
Gateshead Gatesd 43 K5
Gaydon Warwks 22 E5
Gayton Norfk 24 E4
Gedney Drove End
　Lincs 31 K6
Gedney Hill Lincs 31 J8
Georgeham Devon 4 D4
Gerrards Cross Bucks 15 G5
Gifford E Loth 46 F3
Giggleswick N York 37 L6
Gillingham Dorset 13 H8
Gillingham Medway 10 F2
Gillingham Norfk 25 L6
Gilling West N York 38 B3
Gills Highld 65 J1
Gilmerton P & K 50 E4
Gilsland Nthumb 42 E5
Gilwern Mons 21 G8
Girton Cambs 16 C2
Girvan S Ayrs 40 C3
Gisburn Lancs 33 G2
Glamis Angus 51 J3
Glanton Nthumb 47 K7
Glapwell Derbys 30 B3
Glasbury Powys 20 F6
Glasgow C Glas 45 J2
Glaston Rutlnd 23 J1
Glastonbury Somset 12 F7
Glemsford Suffk 17 G3
Glenbarr Ag & B 44 A4
Glenborrodale Highld 52 D5
Glencaple D & G 41 K5
Glencoe Highld 53 H5
Glendaruel Ag & B 49 H5
Glendevon P & K 50 E6
Glenelg Highld 57 H7
Glenfarg P & K 51 G5
Glenfinnan Highld 52 F3
Glenkindie Abers 55 H3
Glenlivet Moray 59 K6
Glenluce D & G 40 C6
Glen Maye IoM 36 b3
Glenridding Cumb 37 G2
Glenrothes Fife 51 H6
Glentham Lincs 35 G7
Glossop Derbys 33 J7
Gloucester Gloucs 21 M7
Glyn Ceiriog Wrexhm 27 K6
Glyncorrwg Neath 19 L6
Glynde E Susx 10 C7
Glynneath Neath 19 L5
Glyntawe Powys 20 C8
Gnosall Staffs 28 F7
Goathland N York 39 H3
Goathurst Somset 12 D7
Gobowen Shrops 27 L6
Godalming Surrey 9 J2
Godmanchester
　Cambs 23 M4
Godshill IoW 8 F7
Goginan Cerdgn 20 B3
Golborne Wigan 32 F6
Goldhanger Essex 17 G6
Golspie Highld 64 E7
Gomshall Surrey 9 K2
Goodwick Pembks 18 C3
Goole E R Yk 34 E4
Goostrey Ches E 28 E3
Gordon Border 47 G5
Gorebridge Mdloth 46 D4
Gorey Jersey 7 c1
Goring Oxon 14 D5
Gorran Haven Cnwll 2 F6
Gorseinon Swans 19 J6
Gosberton Lincs 31 H6
Gosforth Cumb 36 D3
Gosforth N u Ty 43 J5
Gosport Hants 8 F5
Goudhurst Kent 10 F4
Gourock Inver 49 K5
Gowerton Swans 19 J6
Goxhill N Linc 35 H5

Grain Medway 11 G2
Grainthorpe Lincs 35 K6
Grampound Cnwll 2 F6
Gramsdal W Isls 62 d9
Gramsdale W Isls 62 d9
Grandes Rocques
　Guern 6 a1
Grange Cumb 36 F2
Grangemouth Falk 50 E8
Grange-over-Sands
　Cumb 37 G5
Grantham Lincs 30 F6
Grantown-on-Spey
　Highld 59 J6
Grantshouse Border 47 H4
Grasmere Cumb 37 G3
Grassington N York 38 A6
Graveley Herts 16 B4
Gravesend Kent 10 E2
Grays Thurr 10 E3
Great Ayton N York 38 F3
Great Badminton
　S Glos 13 H3
Great Bardfield Essex 16 E4
Great Barford Bed 23 L5
Great Bircham Norfk 24 E3
Great Blakenham
　Suffk 17 J3
Great Casterton
　Rutlnd 30 F8
Great Chesterford
　Essex 16 D3
Great Dalby Leics 30 D7
Great Dunmow Essex 16 E5
Great Durnford Wilts 8 B3
Great Gidding Cambs 23 L3
Great Gransden
　Cambs 16 B2
Greatham Hants 9 H3
Great Harwood
　Lancs 33 G4
Great Haywood
　Staffs 29 G7
Great Hockham
　Norfk 25 G6
Great Kimble Bucks 14 F3
Great Langdale
　Cumb 36 F3
Great Malvern Worcs 21 L5
Great Massingham
　Norfk 24 E4
Great Missenden
　Bucks 14 F4
Great Notley Essex 16 F5
Great Ponton Lincs 30 F6
Great Sampford
　Essex 16 E4
Great Saughall
　Ches W 28 B3
Great Shefford
　W Berk 14 B6
Great Shelford
　Cambs 16 C3
Great Smeaton
　N York 38 D3
Great Tew Oxon 22 E7
Great Torrington
　Devon 4 E5
Great Wakering
　Essex 17 G8
Great Waltham
　Essex 16 E6
Great Witley Worcs 21 L4
Great Yarmouth
　Norfk 25 L5
Great Yeldham Essex 16 F4
Greenfield Flints 27 K3
Green Hammerton
　N York 38 E7
Greenhead Nthumb 42 E5
Greenhow Hill N York 38 B6
Greenlaw Border 47 G5
Greenloaning P & K 50 D6
Greenock Inver 49 L5
Greenodd Cumb 36 F5
Greetham Rutlnd 30 F7
Gresford Wrexhm 27 L4
Greta Bridge Dur 38 B3
Gretna D & G 42 B5
Gretna Green D & G 42 B5
Greystoke Cumb 42 C8
Grimsby NE Lin 35 J5
Grimsthorpe Lincs 31 G7
Grindleford Derbys 29 J3
Gringley on the Hill
　Notts 34 E7
Groby Leics 30 B8
Grosmont Mons 21 H7
Grouville Jersey 7 c2
Grove Oxon 14 B5
Guardbridge Fife 51 J5

Guestling Green
E Susx 11 G6
Guildford Surrey 9 K2
Guisborough R & Cl .. 38 F2
Guiseley Leeds 33 K3
Guist Norfk 25 G4
Gullane E Loth 46 E2
Gunness N Linc 34 E5
Gunnislake Cnwll 3 K4
Gunthorpe Notts 30 D5
Gurnard IoW 8 E6
Gussage All Saints
Dorset 8 A5
Gutcher Shet 61 d2
Guyhirn Cambs 24 B5
Gweek Cnwll 2 D7
Gwernymynydd
Flints 27 K4
Gwithian Cnwll 2 C6
Gwyddelwern
Denbgs 27 J5

H

Hackland Ork 65 b3
Hackness N York 39 J4
Hackney Gt Lon 15 K5
Haddenham Bucks 14 E3
Haddenham Cambs .. 24 C7
Haddington E Loth .. 46 F3
Haddiscoe Norfk 25 L6
Hadleigh Suffk 17 H3
Hadlow Kent 10 E4
Hagworthingham
Lincs 31 J3
Hailsham E Susx 10 E7
Halberton Devon 5 J6
Hales Norfk 25 K6
Halesowen Dudley .. 22 A3
Halesworth Suffk 25 K7
Halifax Calder 33 K4
Halkirk Highld 65 G2
Halstead Essex 16 F4
Halstead Kent 10 D3
Haltwhistle Nthumb .. 42 E5
Halwell Devon 6 B6
Halwill Junction
Devon 4 D7
Hambledon Hants 9 G4
Hamble-le-Rice
Hants 8 E5
Hambleton Lancs 32 D3
Hamilton S Lans 45 K3
Hammersmith Gt Lon .15 J6
Hampstead Norreys
W Berk 14 C6
Hampsthwaite
N York 38 C7
Hamstead Marshall
W Berk 14 B7
Hamstreet Kent 11 H5
Handcross W Susx 10 B5
Handley Ches W 28 C4
Hanley C Stke 28 F5
Happisburgh Norfk .. 25 K3
Harbertonford
Devon 6 B6
Hardwicke Gloucs 13 H1
Hare Street Herts 16 C4
Harewood Leeds 33 L3
Harewood End
Herefs 21 J7
Harlech Gwynd 26 E6
Harleston Norfk 25 J7
Harlosh Highld 56 C5
Harlow Essex 16 C4
Harlyn Cnwll 2 K4
Haroldswick Shet 61 d1
Harpenden Herts 15 H3
Harrogate N York 33 L2
Harrold Bed 23 K5
Harrow Gt Lon 15 H5
Harston Cambs 16 C3
Hartest Suffk 17 G3
Hartfield E Susx 10 D4
Hartington Derbys .. 29 H4
Hartland Devon 4 D4
Hartlepool Hartpl 43 M8
Hartley Wintney
Hants 14 E7
Hartpury Gloucs 21 L7
Harvington Worcs 22 B5
Harwich Essex 17 K4
Haselbury Warwks .. 22 D4
Haslemere Surrey 9 J3
Hastings E Susx 10 F7
Hatch Beauchamp
Somset 12 D4

Hatfield Donc 34 D5
Hatfield Herts 15 J3
Hatfield Broad Oak
Essex 16 D5
Hatfield Heath Essex 16 D5
Hatfield Peverel
Essex 16 F6
Hatherleigh Devon 4 E6
Hathern Leics 30 B7
Hathersage Derbys .. 29 J2
Hatton Abers 61 H5
Havant Hants 9 G5
Havenstreet IoW 8 F6
Haverfordwest
Pembks 18 C5
Haverhill Suffk 16 E3
Hawarden Flints 27 L3
Hawes N York 37 L4
Hawick Border 46 F7
Hawkedon Suffk 16 F3
Hawkhurst Kent 10 F5
Hawkinge Kent 11 K4
Hawkshead Cumb 37 G4
Hawnby N York 38 E4
Haworth C Brad 33 J3
Haxby C York 38 F7
Haxey N Linc 34 E6
Haydon Bridge
Nthumb 42 F5
Hayle Cnwll 2 C6
Hay-on-Wye Powys .. 21 G6
Haywards Heath
W Susx 10 B6
Hazel Grove Stockp .. 28 F2
Heacham Norfk 24 D3
Headcorn Kent 11 G4
Heanor Derbys 29 L5
Heath Derbys 29 L3
Heathfield E Susx 10 E6
Heath Hayes &
Wimblebury
Staffs 29 G8
Hebden Bridge
Calder 33 J4
Heckington Lincs 31 G5
Hedge End Hants 8 E4
Hednesford Staffs .. 29 G8
Hedon E R Yk 35 H4
Helensburgh Ag & B .. 49 L5
Hellifield N York 37 L7
Helmingham Suffk .. 17 K2
Helmsdale Highld 65 G6
Helmsley N York 38 F5
Helpringham Lincs .. 31 G5
Helsby Ches W 28 C3
Helston Cnwll 2 C7
Hemel Hempstead
Herts 15 H3
Hempnall Norfk 25 J6
Hemsby Norfk 25 L4
Hemsworth Wakefd .. 34 B5
Hemyock Devon 5 K6
Hendy Carmth 19 J6
Henfield W Susx 9 L4
Henham Essex 16 D4
Henley-in-Arden
Warwks 22 C4
Henley-on-Thames
Oxon 14 E5
Henllan Denbgs 27 J3
Henlow C Beds 23 L6
Henstead Suffk 25 L7
Henstridge Somset 7 K1
Hereford Herefs 21 J6
Hermitage W Berk .. 14 C6
Herne Bay Kent 11 J2
Hersden Kent 11 K3
Herstmonceux
E Susx 10 E6
Hertford Herts 15 K3
Hessle E R Yk 35 G4
Heswall Wirral 27 L2
Hethersett Norfk 25 H5
Heversham Cumb 37 H5
Hexham Nthumb 43 G5
Hexworthy Devon 3 M4
Heybrook Bay Devon .. 3 K6
Heysham Lancs 37 G7
Heytesbury Wilts 13 J6
Hibaldstow N Linc .. 35 G6
Hickstead W Susx 10 B6
Higham Ferrers
Nhants 23 K4
Highampton Devon 4 E6
High Bentham N York .. 37 J6
Highbridge Somset .. 12 D6
Highclere Hants 14 B7
Higher Town IoS 2 b1
High Halden Kent 11 G5
High Hesket Cumb .. 42 C7

Highley Shrops 21 L3
High Roding Essex .. 16 E5
Highworth Swindn .. 13 M3
High Wycombe
Bucks 14 F4
Hildenborough Kent 10 D4
Hill Brow Hants 9 H3
Hill of Fearn Highld .. 59 G2
Hillswick Shet 61 b3
Hilmarton Wilts 13 K4
Hilton Derbys 29 J6
Hinckley Leics 22 E2
Hinderwell N York .. 39 G2
Hindhead Surrey 9 J3
Hindon Wilts 13 J7
Hingham Norfk 25 G5
Hipswell N York 38 B4
Hirwaun Rhondd 12 A2
Histon Cambs 16 C2
Hitcham Suffk 17 H3
Hitchin Herts 23 M7
Hockley Essex 17 G7
Hockliffe C Beds 23 K7
Hoddesdon Herts 15 K3
Hodnet Shrops 28 D6
Hogsthorpe Lincs 31 L3
Holbeach Lincs 31 J7
Holbeton Devon 3 L5
Holbrook Suffk 17 J4
Holbury Hants 8 E5
Holkham Norfk 24 F2
Hollingbourne Kent .. 11 G3
Holmbury St Mary
Surrey 9 L2
Holmes Chapel
Ches E 28 E3
Holme upon
Spalding Moor
E R Yk 34 E3
Holmfirth Kirk 33 K6
Holmrook Cumb 36 D4
Holne Devon 6 A5
Holsworthy Devon 4 C6
Holt Norfk 25 H3
Holt Wilts 13 H5
Holt Wrexhm 28 B4
Holt Heath Worcs 21 L4
Holton le Clay Lincs 35 J6
Holyhead IoA 26 B2
Holy Island Nthumb 47 L5
Holytown N Lans 45 L2
Holywell Dorset 7 J2
Holywell Flints 27 K3
Homersfield Suffk .. 25 J7
Honingham Norfk .. 25 H5
Honington Suffk 24 F7
Honiton Devon 6 E2
Hook Hants 14 E7
Hoo St Werburgh
Medway 10 F2
Hope Derbys 29 J2
Hope Devon 6 A7
Hope Flints 27 L4
Hope Bowdler
Shrops 21 J2
Hopeman Moray 59 K3
Hope under
Dinmore Herefs 21 J5
Hopton on Sea
Norfk 25 M5
Horam E Susx 10 D6
Horley Surrey 10 B4
Hornby Lancs 37 J6
Horncastle Lincs 31 H3
Horndean Hants 9 G4
Horns Cross Devon 4 D5
Hornsea E R Yk 35 H3
Horrabridge Devon 3 L4
Horsey Norfk 25 L4
Horsham W Susx 9 L3
Horsley Nthumb 43 H5
Horton Dorset 8 B5
Horton Somset 6 F1
Horton-cum-Studley
Oxon 14 D3
Horton-in-
Ribblesdale
N York 37 L6
Horwich Bolton 32 F5
Hoton Leics 30 C7
Houghton-le-Spring
Sundld 43 K6
Houghton on the
Hill Leics 23 G1
Hounslow Gt Lon 15 H6
Houton Ork 65 b4
Hove Br & H. 10 B7
Hovingham N York .. 38 F5
Howden E R Yk 34 E4
Hoxne Suffk 25 J7
Hoylake Wirral 27 J3

Hoyland Nether
Barns 34 B6
Hucknall Notts 30 B5
Huddersfield Kirk .. 33 K5
Hugh Town IoS 2 a2
Hull, Kingston upon
C KuH 35 G4
Humberston NE Lin .. 35 J6
Humbie E Loth 46 E4
Hume Border 47 G5
Hungerford W Berk .. 14 B6
Hunmanby N York .. 39 K5
Hunstanton Norfk .. 24 D2
Huntingdon Cambs 23 M3
Huntley Gloucs 21 L7
Huntly Abers 60 C5
Hursley Hants 8 E4
Hurstbourne Priors
Hants 8 E2
Hurstbourne Tarrant
Hants 14 B7
Hurst Green E Susx .. 10 F5
Hurst Green Lancs .. 32 F3
Hurstpierpoint
W Susx 10 B6
Hurworth-on-Tees
Darltn 38 C3
Husbands Bosworth
Leics 23 G2
Husborne Crawley
C Beds 23 K6
Huttoft Lincs 31 L3
Hutton-le-Hole
N York 39 G4
Hyde Tamesd 33 H7
Hynish Ag & B 48 b3
Hythe Hants 8 E5
Hythe Kent 11 J5

I

Ibstock Leics 29 K8
Ideford Devon 6 C4
Ilchester Somset 12 F8
Ilfracombe Devon 4 E3
Ilkeston Derbys 29 L5
Ilkley C Brad 33 K3
Ilminster Somset 7 G1
Immingham NE Lin .. 35 H5
Immingham Dock
NE Lin. 35 H5
Inchnadamph Highld .. 63 H5
Ingatestone Essex .. 16 E7
Ingham Lincs 30 F2
Ingleton N York 37 K6
Ingoldmells Lincs .. 31 L3
Inkberrow Worcs 22 B5
Innellan Ag & B 49 K6
Innerleithen Border .. 46 D6
Insch Abers 60 D6
Insh Highld 54 C4
Instow Devon 4 D4
Inverallochy Abers .. 61 G3
Inveran Highld 64 C7
Inveraray Ag & B 49 J3
Inverasdale Highld .. 57 H2
Inverbervie Abers .. 55 L6
Invergarry Highld .. 53 K2
Invergordon Highld .. 58 F3
Invergowrie P & K .. 51 H4
Inverinate Highld .. 57 J6
Inverkeilor Angus .. 51 L2
Inverkeithing Fife .. 46 B2
Inverkeithny Abers .. 60 D5
Inverkip Inver 49 K6
Invermoriston Highld .. 58 D7
Inverness Highld 58 F5
Inverurie Abers 55 L3
Ipplepen Devon 6 B5
Ipstones Staffs 29 G5
Ipswich Suffk 17 J3
Irchester Nhants 23 J4
Ireby Cumb 42 A7
Ironbridge Wrekin .. 21 K1
Irthlingborough
Nhants 23 K3
Irvine N Ayrs 45 G4
Isle of Whithorn
D & G. 40 F7
Isleornsay Highld 57 G7
Islington Gt Lon 15 K5
Itchen Abbas Hants .. 8 F3
Iver Bucks 15 G5
Ivinghoe Bucks 15 G3
Ivybridge Devon 3 M5
Iwade Kent 11 G2
Iwerne Minster
Dorset 7 L1
Ixworth Suffk 25 G8

74 Jarrow - Llangernyw

J

Jarrow S Tyne 43 K5
Jedburgh Border 47 G7
Jerbourg Guern 6 b2
Jevington E Susx 10 D7
John o' Groats Highld 65 J1
Johnshaven Abers 55 L7
Johnston Pembks 18 C5
Johnstone Rens 49 M6
Jurby IoM 36 c1

K

Kames Ag & B 49 H6
Keelby Lincs 35 H5
Kegworth Leics 30 B6
Keighley C Brad 33 J3
Keiss Highld 65 J2
Keith Moray 60 B4
Keld N York 37 L3
Kelham Notts 30 D4
Kelso Border 47 G6
Kelvedon Essex 17 G5
Kemble Gloucs 13 K2
Kemnay Abers 55 K3
Kempsey Worcs 21 M5
Kempston Bed 23 K5
Kendal Cumb 37 H4
Kenilworth Warwks 22 D3
Kenmore P & K 50 D3
Kennacraig Ag & B 49 G6
Kennford Devon 6 C3
Kenninghall Norfk 25 G7
Kentallen Highld 53 G5
Kentford Suffk 16 F2
Kenton Devon 6 C4
Kerry Powys 20 F2
Kessingland Suffk 25 L6
Keswick Cumb 36 F2
Kettering Nhants 23 J3
Kettlewell N York 37 M6
Ketton Rutlnd 23 K1
Keymer W Susx 10 B6
Keynsham BaNES 13 G4
Keyston Cambs 23 K3
Keyworth Notts 30 C6
Kibworth Harcourt Leics 23 G2
Kidderminster Worcs 21 M3
Kidlington Oxon 14 C3
Kidsgrove Staffs 28 F4
Kidwelly Carmth 19 G5
Kielder Nthumb 42 D3
Kilberry Ag & B 48 F6
Kilbirnie N Ayrs 45 G3
Kilburn Derbys 29 K5
Kilburn N York 38 E5
Kilchattan Ag & B 44 E3
Kilchoan Highld 52 C4
Kilchrenan Ag & B 49 J2
Kilcreggan Ag & B 49 K5
Kildale N York 38 F3
Kildrummy Abers 55 H3
Kildwick N York 33 J3
Kilfinan Ag & B 49 H5
Kilgetty Pembks 18 E5
Kilham E R Yk 39 K6
Kilkenzie Ag & B 44 B5
Kilkhampton Cnwll 4 C6
Killearn Stirlg 50 B7
Killiecrankie P & K 54 D7
Killin Stirlg 50 B4
Kilmacolm Inver 49 L6
Kilmany Fife 51 J5
Kilmarnock E Ayrs 45 H4
Kilmartin Ag & B 49 G4
Kilmaurs E Ayrs 45 H4
Kilmelford Ag & B 49 G3
Kilmorack Highld 58 D5
Kilninver Ag & B 49 G2
Kilsyth N Lans 50 C8
Kilve Somset 5 K3
Kilwinning N Ayrs 45 G4
Kimberley Norfk 25 H5
Kimbolton Cambs 23 L4
Kinbrace Highld 64 E5
Kincardine Fife 50 E7
Kincardine O'Neil Abers 55 J4
Kincraig Highld 54 C4
Kineton Warwks 22 E5
Kingsbarns Fife 51 K5
Kingsbridge Devon 6 B7
Kingsbury Warwks 22 D2
Kingsclere Hants 14 C7
King's Cliffe Nhants 23 K1
Kingsdown Kent 11 L4
Kingsfold W Susx 9 L3
Kingskerswell Devon 6 C5
Kingsland Herefs 21 H4
Kings Langley Herts 15 H4
Kingsley Staffs 29 G5
King's Lynn Norfk 24 D4
King's Mills Guern 6 a2
Kingsnorth Kent 11 H4
King's Somborne Hants 8 D3
King's Stag Dorset 7 K2
King's Stanley Gloucs 13 H2
Kingsteignton Devon 6 C4
Kingstone Herefs 21 H6
Kingston on Spey Moray 59 L3
Kingston upon Hull C KuH 35 G4
Kingston upon Thames Gt Lon 15 J6
Kingswear Devon 6 C6
Kings Worthy Hants 8 E3
Kington Herefs 21 G5
Kingussie Highld 54 B4
Kinlochbervie Highld 63 H3
Kinlocheil Highld 53 G3
Kinlochewe Highld 57 J3
Kinlochleven Highld 53 J5
Kinloch Rannoch P & K 50 C2
Kinloss Moray 59 J3
Kinmel Bay Conwy 27 H2
Kinneff Abers 55 L6
Kinross P & K 50 F6
Kintbury W Berk 14 B6
Kintore Abers 55 L3
Kippen Stirlg 50 C7
Kirby Misperton N York 39 G5
Kirby Muxloe Leics 22 F1
Kirkabister Shet 61 c6
Kirkbean D & G 41 K6
Kirkbride Cumb 42 A6
Kirkburton Kirk 33 K5
Kirkby Knows 32 D6
Kirkby in Ashfield Notts 30 B4
Kirkby Lonsdale Cumb 37 J5
Kirkby Malzeard N York 38 C5
Kirkbymoorside N York 39 G5
Kirkby Stephen Cumb 37 K3
Kirkcaldy Fife 51 H7
Kirkcolm D & G 40 B5
Kirkconnel D & G 45 K6
Kirkcowan D & G 40 D5
Kirkcudbright D & G 41 G6
Kirkham Lancs 32 D4
Kirkhill Highld 58 E5
Kirkinner D & G 40 E6
Kirkintilloch E Duns 45 K1
Kirk Langley Derbys 29 K6
Kirk Michael IoM 36 b2
Kirkmichael P & K 50 F2
Kirkmichael S Ayrs 45 G6
Kirknewton Nthumb 47 J6
Kirkoswald Cumb 42 D7
Kirkoswald S Ayrs 44 F6
Kirkpatrick-Fleming D & G 42 B5
Kirkton of Skene Abers 55 L4
Kirkwall Ork 65 c4
Kirkwhelpington Nthumb 43 H4
Kirriemuir Angus 51 J2
Kirton Lincs 31 J6
Kirton in Lindsey N Linc 34 F6
Kislingbury Nhants 23 H4
Knaresborough N York 38 D7
Knarsdale Nthumb 42 E6
Knebworth Herts 15 J2
Knighton Powys 21 G3
Knightwick Worcs 21 L5
Knockan Highld 63 H6
Knockin Shrops 27 L7
Knottingley Wakefd 34 C4
Knowl Hill W & M 14 F5
Knutsford Ches E 28 E3
Kyleakin Highld 57 G6
Kyle of Lochalsh Highld 57 G6
Kylerhea Highld 57 G7

L

Laceby NE Lin 35 H6
Ladock Cnwll 2 E5
Ladybank Fife 51 H5
Laggan Highld 54 A5
La Greve de Lecq Jersey 7 a1
Laide Highld 62 E8
Lairg Highld 64 C6
Lakenheath Suffk 24 E7
Lamberhurst Kent 10 E5
Lambourn W Berk 14 B6
Lamerton Devon 3 K3
Lamington S Lans 46 A6
Lamlash N Ayrs 44 D5
Lampeter Cerdgn 19 J2
Lamport Nhants 23 H3
Lanark S Lans 45 M4
Lancaster Lancs 37 H6
Lanchester Dur 43 J6
Lancing W Susx 9 L5
L'Ancresse Guern 6 b1
Landrake Cnwll 3 J5
Langham Rutlnd 30 E8
Langholm D & G 42 B4
Langport Somset 12 E8
Langthwaite N York 38 A3
Langtoft E R Yk 39 J6
Langton Matravers Dorset 8 A7
Langwathby Cumb 42 D7
Langworth Lincs 31 G3
Lanivet Cnwll 3 G4
Lapford Devon 5 G6
Largoward Fife 51 J6
Largs N Ayrs 44 F2
Larkhall S Lans 45 L3
Larkhill Wilts 8 B2
Lastingham N York 39 G4
Latchingdon Essex 17 G7
Latheron Highld 65 H4
Lauder Border 46 F5
Laugharne Carmth 18 F5
Launceston Cnwll 3 J3
Laurencekirk Abers 55 K6
Laurieston D & G 41 G5
Lavenham Suffk 17 G3
Lawers P & K 50 C3
Laxey IoM 36 c3
Laxfield Suffk 25 K8
Lazonby Cumb 42 D7
Leadenham Lincs 30 F5
Leaden Roding Essex 16 E6
Leadgate Dur 43 J6
Leadhills S Lans 45 M6
Leamington Spa Warwks 22 D4
Leatherhead Surrey 15 J7
Lechlade on Thames Gloucs 13 M2
Ledbury Herefs 21 L6
Lee Devon 4 E3
Leebotwood Shrops 21 J1
Leeds Leeds 33 L4
Leek Staffs 29 G4
Leeming Bar N York 38 C4
Lee-on-the-Solent Hants 8 F5
Legbourne Lincs 31 J2
Leicester C Leic 23 G1
Leigh Kent 10 D4
Leigh Wigan 32 F6
Leigh Sinton Worcs 21 L5
Leighton Buzzard C Beds 23 J7
Leintwardine Herefs 21 H3
Leiston Suffk 17 M2
Lelant Cnwll 2 C6
Lendalfoot S Ayrs 40 C3
Lenham Kent 11 G3
Lennoxtown E Duns 50 B8
Leominster Herefs 21 J4
L'Erée Guern 6 a2
Lerwick Shet 61 c6
Leslie Abers 60 D6
Leslie Fife 51 H6
Lesmahagow S Lans 45 L4
Leswalt D & G 40 B5
L'Etacq Jersey 7 a1
Letchworth Garden City Herts 16 B4
Letham Angus 51 K3
Letterston Pembks 18 C4
Leuchars Fife 51 J5
Leven E R Yk 35 H3
Leven Fife 51 J6
Levens Cumb 37 H5
Leverburgh W Isls 62 e7
Lewes E Susx 10 C7
Lewisham Gt Lon 10 C2
Leyburn N York 38 B4
Leyland Lancs 32 E5
Leysdown-on-Sea Kent 11 H2
Lhanbryde Moray 59 L3
Libberton S Lans 46 A5
Lichfield Staffs 29 H8
Lidgate Suffk 16 F2
Lifton Devon 3 J3
Lightwater Surrey 15 G7
Lilliesleaf Border 46 F7
Limpley Stoke Wilts 13 H5
Lincoln Lincs 30 F3
Lindale Cumb 37 G5
Lingfield Surrey 10 C4
Linlithgow W Loth 46 A3
Linton Cambs 16 D3
Linton Kent 10 F4
Liphook Hants 9 H3
Liskeard Cnwll 3 H4
Liss Hants 9 H3
Lissington Lincs 31 G2
Litcham Norfk 24 F4
Litchfield Hants 14 C7
Little Abington Cambs 16 D3
Little Berkhamsted Herts 15 K3
Littleborough Rochdl 33 H5
Little Brickhill M Keyn 23 J6
Little Bytham Lincs 30 F7
Little Clacton Essex 17 J5
Little Gaddesden Herts 15 G3
Littlehampton W Susx 9 K5
Littleport Cambs 24 D6
Little Stretton Shrops 21 H2
Little Torrington Devon 4 E5
Little Walsingham Norfk 25 G3
Liverpool Lpool 32 C7
Livingston W Loth 46 B3
Lizard Cnwll 2 D8
Llanaelhaearn Gwynd 26 C5
Llanarmon Dyffryn Ceiriog Wrexhm 27 K6
Llanarthne Carmth 19 H4
Llanbedr Gwynd 26 E6
Llanbedr-Dyffryn-Clwyd Denbgs 27 K4
Llanbedrog Gwynd 26 C6
Llanberis Gwynd 26 E4
Llanbister Powys 20 F3
Llanbrynmair Powys 20 D1
Llanddarog Carmth 19 H5
Llandderfel Gwynd 27 H6
Llanddulas Conwy 27 H3
Llandeilo Carmth 19 J4
Llandinam Powys 20 E2
Llandissilio Pembks 18 E4
Llandovery Carmth 19 K3
Llandre Cerdgn 20 B2
Llandrillo Denbgs 27 J6
Llandrindod Wells Powys 20 E4
Llandrinio Powys 27 L7
Llandudno Conwy 27 G2
Llandwrog Gwynd 26 D4
Llandybie Carmth 19 J5
Llandysul Cerdgn 19 G3
Llanelli Carmth 19 H6
Llanerchymedd IoA 26 D2
Llanerfyl Powys 27 J8
Llanfachraeth IoA 26 C2
Llanfair Caereinion Powys 27 J8
Llanfair Dyffryn Clwyd Denbgs 27 J4
Llanfairfechan Conwy 26 F3
Llanfair P G IoA 26 D3
Llanfair Talhaiarn Conwy 27 H3
Llanfair Waterdine Shrops 21 G3
Llanfarian Cerdgn 20 A3
Llanfyllin Powys 27 K7
Llangadfan Powys 27 H8
Llangadog Carmth 19 K4
Llangammarch Wells Powys 20 D5
Llangedwyn Powys 27 K7
Llangefni IoA 26 D3
Llangeinor Brdgnd 19 L7
Llangeler Carmth 19 G3
Llangennith Swans 19 G6
Llangernyw Conwy 27 G3

Llangoed IoA 26 E2
Llangollen Denbgs 27 K5
Llangors Powys 20 F7
Llangrannog Cerdgn 18 F2
Llangurig Powys 20 D3
Llangynidr Powys 20 F7
Llangynog Powys 27 J7
Llanhamlach Powys 20 E7
Llanharan Rhondd 12 B3
Llanidloes Powys 20 D2
Llanilar Cerdgn 20 B3
Llanllechid Gwynd 26 E3
Llannefydd Conwy 27 H3
Llanrhaeadr-ym-
  Mochnant Powys 27 J7
Llanrhidian Swans 19 H6
Llanrhystud Cerdgn 20 A4
Llanrug Gwynd 26 E4
Llanrwst Conwy 27 G4
Llansanffraid Glan
  Conwy Conwy 27 G3
Llansannan Conwy 27 H3
Llansantffraid
  Cerdgn 19 H1
Llansantffraid-ym-
  Mechain Powys 27 K7
Llansawel Carmth 19 J3
Llansteffan Carmth 19 G5
Llanthony Mons 21 G7
Llantrisant Rhondd 12 B3
Llantwit Major
  V Glam 5 J1
Llanuwchllyn Gwynd 27 G6
Llanvetherine Mons 21 H8
Llanvihangel
  Crucorney Mons 21 G7
Llanwddyn Powys 27 J7
Llanwnda Gwynd 26 D4
Llanwrda Carmth 19 K3
Llanwrtyd Wells
  Powys 20 D5
Llanybydder Carmth 19 H2
Llanymynech Powys 27 L7
Llanystumdwy
  Gwynd 26 D6
Llay Wrexhm 27 L4
Llechryd Cerdgn 18 F3
Llwyngwril Gwynd 26 E8
Llwynmawr Wrexhm 27 K6
Llynclys Shrops 27 L7
Llyswen Powys 20 F6
Lochailort Highld 52 E3
Lochaline Highld 52 D6
Locharbriggs D & G 41 K4
Lochawe Ag & B 53 H7
Loch Baghasdail
  W Isls 62 c12
Lochboisdale W Isls 62 c12
Lochbuie Ag & B 52 D7
Lochcarron Highld 57 H5
Lochdonhead Ag & B 52 E7
Lochearnhead Stirlg 50 B4
Lochgair Ag & B 49 H4
Lochgilphead Ag & B 49 G4
Lochgoilhead Ag & B 49 K3
Lochinver Highld 63 G5
Lochmaben D & G 41 L4
Lochmaddy W Isls 62 d8
Loch nam Madadh
  W Isls 62 d8
Lochranza N Ayrs 44 D3
Lochwinnoch Rens 45 G2
Lockerbie D & G 41 L4
Lockton N York 39 H4
Loddon Norfk 25 K6
Lofthouse N York 38 B6
Loftus R & Cl 39 G2
London Gt Lon 15 J5
London Colney Herts 15 J4
Long Ashton N Som 12 F4
Long Bennington
  Lincs 30 E5
Long Buckby Nhants 23 G4
Longburton Dorset 7 J1
Long Compton
  Warwks 22 D6
Long Crendon Bucks 14 E3
Long Eaton Derbys 30 B6
Longford Gloucs 21 M7
Longformacus
  Border 47 G4
Longframlington
  Nthumb 43 J2
Longham Dorset 8 B6
Longhorsley Nthumb 43 J3
Longhoughton
  Nthumb 47 M7
Long Itchington
  Warwks 22 E4
Long Lawford
  Warwks 22 F3

Long Marston N York 34 C2
Long Melford Suffk 17 G3
Longniddry E Loth 46 E3
Longnor Shrops 21 J1
Longnor Staffs 29 H4
Long Preston N York 37 L7
Longridge Lancs 32 F3
Longridge W Loth 45 M2
Longside Abers 61 G5
Long Stratton Norfk 25 J6
Long Sutton Lincs 31 K7
Long Sutton Somset 12 F8
Longton Lancs 32 D4
Longtown Cumb 42 B5
Longville in the Dale
  Shrops 21 J2
Looe Cnwll 3 H5
Lossiemouth Moray 59 K3
Lostwithiel Cnwll 3 G5
Loughborough Leics 30 B7
Louth Lincs 31 J2
Lowdham Notts 30 D5
Lower Diabaig Highld 57 H4
Lower Dicker E Susx 10 D6
Lower Peover Ches E 28 E3
Lower Swell Gloucs 22 C7
Lowestoft Suffk 25 M6
Loweswater Cumb 36 K2
Lowick Nhants 23 K3
Lowick Nthumb 47 K5
Low Row N York 37 M4
Lubenham Leics 23 H2
Ludborough Lincs 35 J7
Ludgershall Wilts 8 D2
Ludham Norfk 25 K4
Ludlow Shrops 21 J3
Lugton E Ayrs 45 H3
Lugwardine Herefs 21 J6
Lumphanan Abers 55 J4
Lumsden Abers 55 H3
Lunan Angus 51 L2
Lupton Cumb 37 H5
Luss Ag & B 49 L4
Lusta Highld 56 C4
Luton Luton 15 H2
Lutterworth Leics 22 F2
Lybster Highld 65 H4
Lydbury North
  Shrops 21 H2
Lydd Kent 11 H6
Lydford Devon 6 C7
Lydford on Fosse
  Somset 12 F7
Lydham Shrops 21 G2
Lydney Gloucs 13 G2
Lyme Regis Dorset 7 G3
Lyminge Kent 11 J4
Lymington Hants 8 D6
Lymm Warrtn 28 E2
Lympne Kent 11 J5
Lyndhurst Hants 8 D5
Lyneham Wilts 13 K4
Lyness Ork 65 b5
Lyng Somset 12 E7
Lynmouth Devon 5 G3
Lynton Devon 4 F3
Lyonshall Herefs 21 G5
Lytham St Anne's
  Lancs 32 C4
Lythe N York 39 H3

M

Mablethorpe Lincs 31 K2
Macclesfield Ches E 28 F3
Macduff Abers 60 E3
Machrihanish Ag & B 44 A5
Machynlleth Powys 20 C1
Macmerry E Loth 46 E3
Maentwrog Gwynd 26 F5
Maerdy Rhondd 12 B2
Maesteg Brdgnd 19 L7
Maghull Sefton 32 D6
Maiden Bradley Wilts 13 H7
Maidencombe Torbay 6 C5
Maidenhead W & M 14 F5
Maiden Newton
  Dorset 7 J3
Maidstone Kent 10 F3
Mainsriddle D & G 41 K6
Malborough Devon 6 A7
Maldon Essex 17 G6
Malham N York 37 L6
Mallaig Highld 52 D2
Mallwyd Gwynd 27 G8
Malmesbury Wilts 13 J3
Malpas Ches W 28 C5
Maltby Rothm 34 C7
Malton N York 39 G6

Malvern Wells Worcs 21 L6
Manaccan Cnwll 2 D7
Manchester Manch 33 G6
Manea Cambs 24 C6
Manningtree Essex 17 J4
Manorbier Pembks 18 D6
Mansfield Notts 30 B4
Marazanvose Cnwll 2 E5
Marazion Cnwll 2 B7
March Cambs 24 B6
Marchwiel Wrexhm 28 B5
Marden Kent 10 F4
Mareham le Fen
  Lincs 31 J4
Margaretting Essex 16 E6
Margate Kent 11 L2
Mark Somset 12 E6
Mark Cross E Susx 10 E5
Market Bosworth
  Leics 22 E1
Market Deeping
  Lincs 31 G8
Market Drayton
  Shrops 28 D6
Market Harborough
  Leics 23 H2
Market Lavington
  Wilts 13 K6
Market Rasen Lincs 35 H7
Market Warsop
  Notts 30 C3
Market Weighton
  E R Yk 34 F3
Markfield Leics 30 B8
Markham Moor
  Notts 30 D3
Marksbury BaNES 13 G5
Marks Tey Essex 17 G5
Marlborough Wilts 13 M4
Marloes Pembks 18 B5
Marlow Bucks 14 F5
Marnhull Dorset 7 K1
Marshfield S Glos 13 H4
Marsh Gibbon Bucks 14 D2
Marske-by-the-Sea
  R & Cl 38 F2
Martin Lincs 31 G4
Martinstown Dorset 7 J3
Martlesham Heath
  Suffk 17 K3
Martock Somset 7 H1
Marton Warwks 22 E4
Marykirk Abers 55 K7
Maryport Cumb 41 K7
Mary Tavy Devon 3 L3
Marywell Abers 55 J5
Masham N York 38 C5
Matfield Kent 10 E4
Matlock Derbys 29 K4
Mattingley Hants 14 E7
Mauchline E Ayrs 45 H5
Maud Abers 60 F4
Maughold IoM 36 d2
Maulden C Beds 23 K6
Mawgan Porth Cnwll 2 E4
Mawnan Smith Cnwll 2 D7
Maybole S Ayrs 44 E6
Mayfield E Susx 10 E5
Mayfield Staffs 29 H5
Meare Somset 12 F6
Measham Leics 29 K8
Medstead Hants 9 G3
Meeth Devon 4 E6
Meifod Powys 27 K8
Meigle P & K 51 H3
Melbourn Cambs 16 C3
Melbourne Derbys 29 K7
Meliden Denbgs 27 J2
Melksham Wilts 13 J5
Melling Lancs 37 J6
Melmerby Cumb 42 D7
Melrose Border 46 F6
Meltham Kirk 33 K5
Melton E R Yk 34 F4
Melton Constable
  Norfk 25 H3
Melton Mowbray
  Leics 30 D7
Melvaig Highld 57 G2
Melvich Highld 64 E2
Memsie Abers 61 G3
Memus Angus 51 J2
Menai Bridge IoA 26 E3
Mentmore Bucks 14 F2
Meopham Kent 10 E2
Mere Wilts 13 H7
Meriden Solhll 22 D2
Merthyr Tydfil Myr Td 12 B2
Merton Devon 4 E6
Messingham N Linc 34 F6
Metfield Suffk 25 K7

Methil Fife 51 J6
Methlick Abers 60 F5
Methven P & K 50 F4
Methwold Norfk 24 E6
Mevagissey Cnwll 2 F6
Mexborough Donc 34 B6
Miabhig W Isls 62 f3
Miavaig W Isls 62 f3
Micheldever Hants 8 F2
Mickleton Dur 37 M2
Mickleton Gloucs 22 C6
Midbea Ork 65 c2
Middleham N York 38 B4
Middle Rasen Lincs 35 G7
Middlesbrough
  Middsb 38 E2
Middleton Cheney
  Nhants 22 F6
Middleton-in-
  Teesdale Dur 37 M2
Middleton-on-Sea
  W Susx 9 J5
Middleton on the
  Wolds E R Yk 34 F2
Middleton Stoney
  Oxon 14 C2
Middle Town IoS 2 a2
Middle Wallop Hants 8 D3
Middlewich Ches E 28 E3
Middlezoy Somset 12 E7
Midhurst W Susx 9 J4
Midsomer Norton
  BaNES 13 G6
Mid Yell Shet 61 d2
Milborne Port
  Somset 7 J1
Mildenhall Suffk 24 E7
Milfield Nthumb 47 J6
Milford Haven
  Pembks 18 C5
Milford on Sea Hants 8 D6
Millbrook Cnwll 3 K5
Millbrook Jersey 7 b2
Millom Cumb 36 E5
Millport N Ayrs 44 F3
Milnathort P & K 50 F6
Milngavie E Duns 45 J1
Milton Abbas Dorset 7 K2
Milton Abbot Devon 3 K3
Milton Damerel
  Devon 4 D6
Milton Ernest Bed 23 K5
Milton Keynes
  M Keyn 23 J4
Milverton Somset 5 K5
Minchinhampton
  Gloucs 13 J2
Minehead Somset 5 J3
Minster Kent 11 H2
Minster Kent 11 L2
Minsterley Shrops 28 B8
Minster Lovell Oxon 14 A3
Mintlaw Abers 61 G4
Mirfield Kirk 33 K5
Misterton Notts 34 E7
Misterton Somset 7 H2
Mitcheldean Gloucs 21 K7
Mobberley Ches E 28 E2
Mochrum D & G 40 E6
Modbury Devon 3 M5
Moffat D & G 41 L2
Mold Flints 27 K4
Moniaive D & G 41 H3
Monifieth Angus 51 K4
Monkleigh Devon 4 D5
Monkton S Ayrs 45 G5
Monmouth Mons 21 J8
Montacute Somset 7 H1
Montford Bridge
  Shrops 28 B7
Montgomery Powys 20 F1
Montrose Angus 51 L2
Mont Saint Guern 6 a2
Monyash Derbys 29 H3
Monymusk Abers 55 K3
Morchard Bishop
  Devon 5 G6
Morcott Rutlnd 23 J1
Mordiford Herefs 21 J6
Morebattle Border 47 H7
Morecambe Lancs 37 G6
Moreton Dorset 7 K3
Moretonhampstead
  Devon 6 B3
Moreton-in-Marsh
  Gloucs 22 C6
Morfa Nefyn Gwynd 26 B5
Morley Leeds 33 L4
Morpeth Nthumb 43 J3
Morston Norfk 25 G2
Mortehoe Devon 4 D3

Mortimer W Berk 14 D7
Morville Shrops 21 K2
Morwenstow Cnwll 4 B5
Mossat Abers 55 H3
Mosstodloch Moray .. 59 L4
Mosterton Dorset 7 H2
Mostyn Flints 27 K2
Motherby Cumb 37 G1
Motherwell N Lans .. 45 K3
Moulsford Oxon 14 D5
Moulton Nhants 23 H4
Mountain Ash
    Rhondd 12 B2
Mountsorrel Leics 30 C7
Mousehole Cnwll 2 B7
Moy Highld 58 F5
Muchalls Abers 55 M5
Much Birch Herefs 21 J7
Much Hadham Herts .. 16 C5
Much Marcle Herefs .. 21 K6
Much Wenlock
    Shrops 21 K1
Muddiford Devon 4 E4
Muirdrum Angus 51 K3
Muirhead Angus 51 H4
Muirkirk E Ayrs 45 K5
Muir of Ord Highld .. 58 D4
Muker N York 37 L4
Mullion Cnwll 2 D8
Mundesley Norfk 25 K3
Mundford Norfk 24 E6
Mungrisdale Cumb .. 42 B8
Munlochy Highld 58 E4
Munslow Shrops 21 J2
Musselburgh E Loth .. 46 D3
Muthill P & K 50 D5

N

Nacton Suffk 17 K4
Nailsea N Som 12 F4
Nailsworth Gloucs 13 J2
Nairn Highld 59 G4
Nantgaredig Carmth .. 19 H4
Nantwich Ches E 28 D5
Narberth Pembks 18 E5
Narborough Norfk 24 E4
Naseby Nhants 23 G3
Navenby Lincs 30 F4
Nayland Suffk 17 H4
Nazeing Essex 16 C6
Neath Neath 19 K6
Necton Norfk 24 F5
Needham Market
    Suffk 17 J2
Nefyn Gwynd 26 C5
Nelson Lancs 33 H3
Nesscliffe Shrops 28 B7
Neston Ches W 27 L3
Nether Stowey
    Somset 12 C7
Nether Wasdale
    Cumb 36 E3
Nethy Bridge Highld .. 54 D3
Nettlebed Oxon 14 E5
Nevern Pembks 18 E3
New Abbey D & G 41 K5
New Aberdour Abers .. 60 F3
New Alresford Hants .. 8 F3
Newark-on-Trent
    Notts 30 E4
Newarthill N Lans 45 L2
Newbiggin Dur 37 L1
Newbiggin N York 38 A5
Newbiggin-by-the-
    Sea Nthumb 43 K4
Newbigging S Lans .. 46 A5
Newbold on Stour
    Warwks 22 D5
New Bolingbroke
    Lincs 31 J4
Newborough IoA 26 D4
Newbridge Caerph .. 12 C2
Newbridge D & G 41 K4
Newbridge on Wye
    Powys 20 E4
New Buckenham
    Norfk 25 H6
Newburgh Abers 61 G6
Newburgh Fife 51 G5
Newbury W Berk 14 C6
Newby Bridge Cumb .. 37 G5
Newcastle Emlyn
    Carmth 18 F3
Newcastleton Border .. 42 C3
Newcastle-under-
    Lyme Staffs 28 F5
Newcastle upon
    Tyne N u Ty 43 K5

New Cumnock E Ayrs .. 45 J6
New Deer Abers 60 F5
Newent Gloucs 21 L7
Newgale Pembks 18 C4
New Galloway D & G .. 41 G4
New Grimsby IoS 2 a1
Newhaven E Susx 10 C7
New Holland N Linc .. 35 G4
Newick E Susx 10 C6
New Luce D & G 40 C5
Newlyn Cnwll 2 B7
Newmains N Lans .. 45 L3
Newmarket Suffk 16 E2
Newmill Moray 60 B4
New Milton Hants 8 C6
Newnham Gloucs 13 G1
Newnham Worcs 21 K4
New Pitsligo Abers .. 60 F4
Newport Essex 16 D4
Newport IoW 8 F7
Newport Newpt 12 D3
Newport Pembks 18 D3
Newport Wrekin 28 E7
Newport-on-Tay Fife .. 51 J4
Newport Pagnell
    M Keyn 23 J6
New Quay Cerdgn .. 19 G1
Newquay Cnwll 2 E5
New Radnor Powys .. 20 F4
New Romney Kent .. 11 H5
Newsham N York 38 B3
Newton Abbot
    Devon 6 C5
Newton Aycliffe Dur .. 38 C2
Newton Ferrers
    Devon 3 L6
Newton Ferry W Isls .. 62 d8
Newtongrange
    Mdloth 46 D4
Newton Mearns
    E Rens 45 J3
Newtonmore Highld .. 54 B4
Newton-on-the-
    Moor Nthumb 43 J2
Newton on Trent
    Lincs 30 E3
Newton St Cyres
    Devon 6 C3
Newton Solney
    Derbys 29 J7
Newton Stewart
    D & G 40 E5
Newtown Herefs 21 K5
Newtown Powys 20 F2
New Tredegar
    Caerph 12 C2
Newtyle Angus 51 H3
Neyland Pembks 18 D5
Nigg Highld 59 G3
Ninfield E Susx 10 E6
Niton IoW 8 F7
Nocton Lincs 31 G4
Norham Nthumb 47 J5
Normanton Wakefd .. 34 B4
Northall Bucks 15 G2
Northallerton N York .. 38 D4
Northam Devon 4 D4
Northampton
    Nhants 23 H4
North Berwick
    E Loth 46 F2
North Cave E R Yk .. 34 F4
Northchapel W Susx .. 9 J3
North Chideock
    Dorset 7 G3
North Cotes Lincs 35 K6
North Creake Norfk .. 24 F3
North Curry Somset .. 12 D8
North Dalton E R Yk .. 34 F2
North Elmham Norfk .. 25 G4
North Ferriby E R Yk .. 35 G4
Northfleet Kent 10 E2
North Frodingham
    E R Yk 35 H2
North Grimston
    N York 39 H6
North Hayling Hants .. 9 G5
North Hykeham
    Lincs 30 F3
Northiam E Susx 11 G6
North Kessock
    Highld 58 F4
North Kilworth Leics .. 30 C7
North Kyme Lincs 31 H4
Northleach Gloucs .. 22 C8
North Luffenham
    Rutlnd 23 J7
North Molton Devon .. 5 G4
North Muskham
    Notts 30 E4
Northop Flints 27 K3

North Petherton
    Somset 12 D7
North Rigton N York .. 33 L2
North Shields
    N Tyne 43 K5
North Somercotes
    Lincs 35 K6
North Walsham
    Norfk 25 J3
North Waltham
    Hants 8 F2
North Weald Bassett
    Essex 16 D6
Northwich Ches W .. 28 D3
North Wingfield
    Derbys 29 K4
Northwold Norfk 24 E6
Norton-on-Derwent
    N York 39 G6
Norton St Philip
    Somset 13 H5
Norwich Norfk 25 J5
Nottingham C Nott .. 30 C5
Nuneaton Warwks .. 22 E2
Nunney Somset 13 H6
Nutley E Susx 10 C5

O

Oadby Leics 23 G1
Oakham Rutlnd 30 E8
Oakhill Somset 13 G6
Oakley Bed 23 K5
Oakley Bucks 14 D3
Oakley Hants 8 F2
Oare Wilts 13 L5
Oban Ag & B 52 F7
Ochiltree E Ayrs 45 H5
Ockbrook Derbys 29 L6
Ockley Surrey 9 L2
Odiham Hants 9 G2
Offenham Worcs 22 B5
Ogbourne St George
    Wilts 13 M4
Ogmore-by-Sea
    V Glam 19 L8
Okehampton Devon .. 4 E7
Old Deer Abers 61 G4
Old Grimsby IoS 2 a1
Oldham Oldham 33 H6
Old Hurst Cambs 24 A7
Old Leake Lincs 31 K5
Oldmeldrum Abers .. 60 F6
Old Rayne Abers 60 D6
Old Sodbury S Glos .. 13 H3
Old Stratford
    Nhants 23 H6
Old Town IoS 2 b2
Old Windsor W & M .. 15 G6
Ollaberry Shet 61 b3
Ollerton Notts 30 C3
Olney M Keyn 23 J5
Ombersley Worcs 21 M4
Onchan IoM 36 C3
Onich Highld 53 G5
Orford Suffk 17 L3
Ormesby St
    Margaret Norfk .. 25 L4
Ormskirk Lancs 32 D6
Orpington Gt Lon 10 D2
Orsett Thurr 10 E1
Orton Cumb 37 J3
Osbournby Lincs 31 G6
Osmington Dorset .. 7 K4
Osmotherley N York .. 38 E4
Ospringe Kent 11 H3
Ossett Wakefd 33 L5
Oswaldkirk N York .. 38 F5
Oswestry Shrops 27 L6
Otford Kent 10 D3
Othery Somset 12 E7
Otley Leeds 33 K3
Otterbourne Hants .. 8 E4
Otterburn Nthumb .. 43 G3
Otter Ferry Ag & B .. 49 H5
Ottershaw Surrey 15 G7
Otterton Devon 6 E4
Ottery St Mary
    Devon 6 E3
Oundle Nhants 23 K2
Outwell Norfk 24 C5
Overseal Derbys 29 K7
Overton Hants 8 F2
Overton Wrexhm .. 28 B5
Ower Hants 8 D4
Oxford Oxon 14 C3
Oxted Surrey 10 C3
Oxton Notts 30 C5
Oxwich Swans 19 H7

P

Padbury Bucks 23 H7
Paddock Wood Kent .. 10 E4
Padiham Lancs 33 G4
Padstow Cnwll 2 F4
Paignton Torbay 6 C5
Pailton Warwks 22 F3
Painswick Gloucs 13 J1
Paisley Rens 45 H2
Palnackie D & G 41 J6
Pandy Mons 21 G7
Pangbourne W Berk .. 14 D6
Pannal N York 33 L2
Pant-y-dwr Powys .. 20 E3
Papworth Everard
    Cambs 16 B2
Parracombe Devon .. 4 F3
Pateley Bridge
    N York 38 B6
Patna E Ayrs 45 H6
Patrick IoM 36 b3
Patrington E R Yk .. 35 J4
Patterdale Cumb 37 G2
Pattishall Nhants 23 G5
Peacehaven E Susx .. 10 C7
Peasedown St John
    BaNES 13 H5
Peasmarsh E Susx .. 11 G6
Peebles Border 46 C5
Peel IoM 36 b3
Pelynt Cnwll 3 H5
Pembrey Carmth 19 G6
Pembridge Herefs .. 21 H4
Pembroke Pembks .. 18 D6
Pembroke Dock
    Pembks 18 D6
Pembury Kent 10 E4
Penally Pembks 18 E6
Penarth V Glam 12 C4
Pencoed Brdgnd 12 A3
Pencraig Herefs 21 J7
Pendine Carmth 18 F5
Pendock Worcs 21 L6
Pendoggett Cnwll 3 G3
Pengam Caerph 12 C2
Penicuik Mdloth 46 C4
Penistone Barns 33 L6
Penkridge Staffs 29 G7
Penmachno Conwy .. 27 G5
Penmaenmawr
    Conwy 26 F3
Pennal Gwynd 20 B1
Pennan Abers 60 F3
Penpont D & G 41 J3
Penrhyndeudraeth
    Gwynd 26 E6
Penrith Cumb 42 D8
Penryn Cnwll 2 E7
Pensford BaNES 13 G5
Penshurst Kent 10 D4
Pensilva Cnwll 3 J4
Pentewan Cnwll 2 F6
Pentraeth IoA 26 D3
Pentrefoelas Conwy .. 27 G5
Penybont Powys 20 F4
Pen-y-bont-fawr
    Powys 27 J7
Penygroes Gwynd .. 26 D4
Penzance Cnwll 2 B7
Perranporth Cnwll .. 2 D5
Pershore Worcs 22 A5
Perth P & K 50 F4
Peterborough C Pete .. 23 M1
Peterchurch Herefs .. 21 H6
Peterculter C Aber .. 55 L4
Peterhead Abers 61 H5
Peterlee Dur 43 L7
Petersfield Hants 9 H4
Petton Devon 5 J5
Petworth W Susx 9 J4
Pevensey E Susx 10 E7
Pewsey Wilts 13 L5
Pickering N York 39 G5
Piercebridge Darltn .. 38 C2
Pierowall Ork 65 c1
Pillaton Cnwll 3 J4
Pillerton Priors
    Warwks 22 D5
Pilling Lancs 32 D3
Pinchbeck Lincs 31 H6
Pinwherry S Ayrs 40 C3
Pinxton Derbys 29 L4
Pirbright Surrey 15 G7
Pitcaple Abers 60 E6
Pitlochry P & K 50 E2
Pitmedden Abers 60 F6
Pittenweem Fife 51 K6
Pleasley Derbys 30 B4
Plockton Highld 57 H6

Pluckley Kent...............11 G4
Plumpton E Susx............10 C6
Plumtree Notts..............30 C6
Plymouth C Plym.............3 K5
Plympton C Plym.............3 L5
Pocklington E R Yk.........34 E2
Polbathic Cnwll.............3 J5
Polegate E Susx............10 D7
Polmont Falk...............50 E8
Polperro Cnwll..............3 H5
Polruan Cnwll...............3 G5
Polzeath Cnwll..............2 F3
Pontardawe Neath..........19 K6
Pontarddulais Swans.......19 J6
Pontefract Wakefd.........34 B5
Ponteland Nthumb..........43 J4
Ponterwyd Cerdgn..........20 C3
Pontesbury Shrops.........28 B8
Pontlanfraith
  Caerph..................12 C2
Pontrhydfendigaid
  Cerdgn..................19 K1
Pontrilas Herefs...........21 H7
Pontyates Carmth..........19 H5
Pontyberem Carmth.........19 H5
Pontypool Torfn............12 D2
Pontypridd Rhondd.........12 B3
Pool Leeds.................33 L3
Poole Poole.................8 A6
Poolewe Highld.............57 H2
Pooley Bridge Cumb........37 H2
Porlock Somset..............5 H3
Porlock Weir Somset........5 H3
Port Appin Ag & B.........52 F6
Port Askaig Ag & B........48 D6
Portavadie Ag & B.........49 H6
Port Bannatyne
  Ag & B..................49 J6
Port Carlisle Cumb........42 A5
Port Charlotte
  Ag & B..................48 B7
Portchester Hants..........8 F5
Port Ellen Ag & B.........48 C8
Port Erin IoM..............36 a4
Portesham Dorset...........7 J3
Port Eynon Swans..........19 H7
Port Glasgow Inver........49 L5
Portgordon Moray..........60 B3
Porth Rhondd...............12 B3
Porthcawl Brdgnd..........19 L8
Porthcothan Cnwll..........2 E4
Porthcurno Cnwll...........2 A8
Port Henderson
  Highld..................57 G3
Porthleven Cnwll...........2 C7
Porthmadog Gwynd.........26 E6
Porthtowan Cnwll...........2 D6
Portinscale Cumb..........36 F2
Port Isaac Cnwll...........2 F3
Portishead N Som..........12 F4
Portknockie Moray.........60 C3
Portlethen Abers..........55 M5
Portloe Cnwll...............2 F6
Port Logan D & G..........40 C7
Portmahomack
  Highld..................59 H2
Portnacroish Ag & B.......53 G6
Portnahaven Ag & B........48 A7
Port nan Long W Isls......62 d8
Port Nis W Isls............62 i1
Port of Menteith
  Stirlg..................50 B6
Port of Ness W Isls.......62 i1
Portpatrick D & G.........40 B6
Portreath Cnwll............2 C6
Portree Highld.............56 E5
Port St Mary IoM..........36 a4
Portscatho Cnwll...........2 E7
Portskerra Highld.........64 E2
Portslade-by-Sea
  Br & H..................10 B7
Portsmouth C Port..........9 G5
Portsoy Abers..............60 D3
Port Talbot Neath.........19 K7
Port William D & G........40 E7
Postbridge Devon...........3 M3
Postcombe Oxon............14 E4
Potterne Wilts.............13 K5
Potters Bar Herts.........15 J4
Potton C Beds..............16 B3
Poulton-le-Fylde
  Lancs...................32 C3
Powburn Nthumb............47 K7
Powick Worcs...............21 M5
Poynton Ches E.............28 F2
Praa Sands Cnwll...........2 C7
Prees Shrops...............28 C6
Preesall Lancs.............32 D3
Prees Green Shrops........28 C6
Prenteg Gwynd..............26 E5
Prestatyn Denbgs..........27 J2

Prestbury Ches E...........28 F3
Presteigne Powys..........21 G4
Preston Border.............47 H4
Preston Lancs..............32 E4
Preston Candover
  Hants....................8 F2
Preston Capes
  Nhants..................22 F5
Prestonpans E Loth........46 E3
Prestwich Bury.............33 G6
Prestwick S Ayrs..........45 G5
Prestwood Bucks...........14 F4
Priddy Somset..............12 F6
Princes Risborough
  Bucks...................14 F4
Princethorpe Warwks.......22 E3
Princetown Devon...........3 L4
Prospect Cumb..............41 L7
Prudhoe Nthumb............43 H5
Pucklechurch S Glos.......13 H4
Puddletown Dorset..........7 K3
Pudsey Leeds...............33 L4
Pulborough W Susx..........9 K4
Pulford Ches W.............28 B4
Pulham St Mary
  Norfk...................25 J7
Pumsaint Carmth...........19 J3
Purfleet Thurr.............10 D1
Purton Wilts...............13 L3
Pwll Carmth................19 H6
Pwllheli Gwynd.............26 C6
Pyecombe W Susx...........10 B6
Pyle Brdgnd................19 L7

Q

Quatt Shrops...............21 L2
Queensferry Flints........27 L3
Quendon Essex..............16 D4

R

Rackenford Devon...........5 H5
Rackheath Norfk............25 J4
Radcliffe on Trent
  Notts...................30 C6
Radlett Herts..............15 H4
Radstock BaNES.............13 G5
Radwinter Essex............16 E4
Radyr Cardif...............12 C4
Rafford Moray..............59 J4
Raglan Mons................12 E1
Rainham Gt Lon.............10 D1
Rampside Cumb..............36 F6
Ramsbury Wilts.............14 A6
Ramsey Cambs...............24 A7
Ramsey IoM.................36 c2
Ramsgate Kent..............11 L2
Rannoch Station
  P & K...................53 L5
Rapness Ork................65 c2
Rathen Abers...............61 G3
Raunds Nhants..............23 K3
Ravenglass Cumb...........36 E4
Ravenscar N York..........39 J3
Ravenstonedale
  Cumb....................37 K3
Rawmarsh Rothm............34 B7
Rawtenstall Lancs.........33 G4
Rayleigh Essex.............16 F7
Reading Readg..............14 E6
Reay Highld................64 F2
Reculver Kent..............11 K2
Redbourn Herts............15 H3
Redbrook Gloucs...........12 F1
Redbrook Wrexhm...........28 C5
Redcar R & Cl.............38 F2
Redditch Worcs............22 B4
Redgrave Suffk............25 G7
Redhill N Som.............12 F5
Redhill Surrey............10 B4
Redmile Leics.............30 E6
Rednal Shrops.............28 B6
Red Roses Carmth..........18 F5
Red Row Nthumb............43 K2
Redruth Cnwll..............2 D6
Red Wharf Bay IoA.........26 D2
Reedham Norfk.............25 L5
Reepham Norfk.............25 H4
Reigate Surrey............10 B4
Reighton N York...........39 K5
Rempstone Notts...........30 C7
Renfrew Rens...............45 H2
Renwick Cumb...............42 D7
Repton Derbys.............29 K6
Resolven Neath............19 L6
Retford Notts.............30 D2

Reynoldston Swans.........19 H7
Rhayader Powys............20 D4
Rhiconich Highld..........63 H3
Rhoose V Glam..............5 J2
Rhoslanerchrugog
  Wrexhm..................27 L5
Rhosneigr IoA.............26 C3
Rhôs-on-Sea Conwy.........27 G2
Rhossili Swans............19 G7
Rhu Ag & B.................49 L5
Rhuddlan Denbgs...........27 J3
Rhyd-Ddu Gwynd............26 E4
Rhydowen Cerdgn...........19 G2
Rhyl Denbgs................27 H2
Rhymney Caerph............12 C1
Richards Castle
  Herefs..................21 J4
Richmond Gt Lon...........15 J6
Richmond N York...........38 B3
Rickmansworth
  Herts...................15 H4
Riding Mill Nthumb........43 H5
Ridsdale Nthumb...........43 G4
Rillington N York.........39 H5
Ringford D & G............41 G6
Ringmer E Susx............10 C6
Ringwood Hants.............8 C5
Ripley Derbys.............29 K5
Ripley N York.............38 C2
Ripley Surrey.............15 H7
Ripon N York..............38 D6
Ripple Worcs..............21 M6
Ripponden Calder.........33 J5
Risca Caerph..............12 D3
Risegate Lincs............31 H6
Riseley Bed...............23 K4
Riseley Wokham............14 E7
Risley Derbys.............29 L6
Risley Warrtn.............32 F7
Roade Nhants..............23 H5
Roberton Border...........46 E7
Roberton S Lans...........45 M5
Robertsbridge E Susx......10 F6
Robeston Wathen
  Pembks..................18 E5
Robin Hood's Bay
  N York..................39 J3
Rocester Staffs...........29 H6
Roch Pembks...............18 C4
Rochdale Rochdl...........33 H5
Roche Cnwll................2 F5
Rochester Medway..........10 F2
Rochester Nthumb..........42 F3
Rochford Essex............17 G7
Rock Cnwll.................2 F3
Rockcliffe Cumb...........42 B5
Rockcliffe D & G..........41 J6
Rockingham Nhants.........23 J2
Rogate W Susx..............9 H4
Rogerstone Newpt..........12 D3
Rollesby Norfk............25 L4
Rolvenden Kent............11 G5
Romaldkirk Dur............37 M2
Romanno Bridge
  Border..................46 C5
Romford Gt Lon............16 D7
Romsey Hants...............8 D4
Rookhope Dur..............43 G7
Ropley Hants...............9 G3
Rosedale Abbey
  N York..................39 G4
Rosehall Highld...........63 K7
Rosehearty Abers..........61 G3
Rosemarkie Highld.........58 F4
Rosewell Mdloth...........46 D4
Rossett Wrexhm............28 B4
Ross-on-Wye Herefs........21 K7
Rosyth Fife...............46 B2
Rothbury Nthumb...........43 H2
Rotherfield E Susx........10 D5
Rotherham Rothm...........34 B7
Rothes Moray..............59 L4
Rothesay Ag & B...........49 J6
Rothwell Leeds............33 M4
Rothwell Nhants...........23 H3
Rottingdean Br & H........10 C7
Roughton Norfk............25 J3
Rowland's Castle
  Hants....................9 G5
Rowland's Gill Gatesd.....43 J4
Rowsley Derbys............29 J3
Roxburgh Border...........47 G6
Roxwell Essex.............16 E6
Royal Leamington
  Spa Warwks..............22 D4
Royal Sutton
  Coldfield Birm..........22 C2
Royal Tunbridge
  Wells Kent..............10 E4
Royal Wootton
  Bassett Wilts...........13 L3

Royston Barns.............34 A5
Royston Herts.............16 C4
Rozel Jersey...............7 c1
Ruabon Wrexhm.............27 L5
Ruddington Notts..........30 C6
Rudgwick W Susx............9 K3
Rudston E R Yk............39 K6
Rufford Lancs.............32 D5
Rugby Warwks..............22 F3
Rugeley Staffs............29 G7
Rumbling Bridge
  P & K...................50 F6
Runcorn Halton............28 C2
Rushden Nhants............23 K4
Rushyford Dur.............38 C1
Ruskington Lincs..........31 G5
Rustington W Susx..........9 K5
Ruswarp N York............39 H3
Rutherglen S Lans.........45 J2
Ruthin Denbgs.............27 J4
Ruyton-XI-Towns
  Shrops..................28 B7
Rydal Cumb................37 G3
Ryde IoW...................8 F6
Rye E Susx................11 G6

S

Saddell Ag & B............44 B5
Saffron Walden
  Essex...................16 D4
St Abbs Border............47 J3
St Agnes Cnwll.............2 D5
St Albans Herts...........15 H3
St Andrew Guern............6 a2
St Andrews Fife...........51 K5
St Arvans Mons............12 F2
St Asaph Denbgs...........27 J3
St Athan V Glam............5 J1
St Aubin Jersey...........7 b2
St Austell Cnwll...........2 F5
St Bees Cumb..............36 D3
St Blazey Cnwll............3 G5
St Boswells Border........46 F6
St Brelade Jersey..........7 a2
St Brelade's Bay
  Jersey...................7 a2
St Briavels Gloucs........12 F2
St Buryan Cnwll............2 A7
St Catherines Ag & B......49 J3
St Clears Carmth..........18 F5
St Cleer Cnwll.............3 H4
St Clement Jersey..........7 c2
St Columb Major
  Cnwll....................2 F4
St Combs Abers............61 H3
St Cyrus Abers............55 K7
St Davids Pembks..........18 B4
St Day Cnwll...............2 D6
St Dogmaels Pembks........18 E2
St Fergus Abers...........61 H4
St Fillans P & K..........50 C4
St Florence Pembks........18 E6
St Helens IoW..............9 G6
St Helens St Hel..........32 E7
St Helier Jersey..........7 b2
St Ives Cambs.............24 A8
St Ives Cnwll..............2 B6
St John Jersey............7 b1
St John's IoM.............36 b3
St John's Chapel Dur......43 G7
St John's Town of
  Dalry D & G.............41 G4
St Jude's IoM.............36 c2
St Just Cnwll..............2 A7
St Just-in-Roseland
  Cnwll....................2 E7
St Keverne Cnwll...........2 E8
St Keyne Cnwll.............3 H5
St Lawrence IoW............8 F7
St Lawrence Jersey........7 b1
St Margaret's at
  Cliffe Kent.............11 L4
St Margaret's Hope
  Ork.....................65 c5
St Marks IoM..............36 b3
St Martin Guern............6 b2
St Martin Jersey..........7 c1
St Mary Jersey............7 b1
St Mary's Ork.............65 c4
St Mary's Bay Kent........11 J5
St Mawes Cnwll.............2 E7
St Monans Fife............51 K6
St Neots Cambs............23 M4
St Osyth Essex............17 J5
St Ouen Jersey............7 a1
St Owens Cross
  Herefs..................21 J7

St Peter Jersey....7 b1
St Peter Port Guern....6 b2
St Peter's Guern....6 a2
St Sampson Guern....6 b1
St Saviour Guern....6 a2
St Saviour Jersey....7 b2
St Stephen Cnwll....2 F5
St Tudy Cnwll....3 G3
Salcombe Devon....6 B7
Sale Traffd....33 G7
Salen Ag & B....52 D6
Salen Highld....52 E4
Salfords Surrey....10 B4
Saline Fife....50 F7
Salisbury Wilts....8 C3
Saltash Cnwll....3 K5
Saltburn-by-the-Sea R & Cl....38 F2
Saltcoats N Ayrs....44 F6
Saltfleet Lincs....35 K7
Sampford Arundel Somset....5 K5
Sampford Brett Somset....5 J3
Sanaigmore Ag & B....48 B6
Sandbach Ches E....28 E4
Sandbank Ag & B....49 K5
Sandford-on-Thames Oxon....14 C4
Sandhaven Abers....61 G3
Sandhead D & G....40 C6
Sandhurst Br For....14 F7
Sandness Shet....61 a5
Sandon Staffs....29 G6
Sandown IoW....8 F7
Sandridge Herts....15 J3
Sandsend N York....39 H3
Sandwich Kent....11 L3
Sandwick Shet....61 c7
Sandy C Beds....23 L5
Sanquhar D & G....45 L6
Sarn Gwynd....26 B6
Sarre Kent....11 K2
Saundby Notts....34 E7
Saundersfoot Pembks....18 E5
Saunton Devon....4 D4
Sawbridgeworth Herts....16 D5
Sawston Cambs....16 D3
Sawtry Cambs....23 L3
Saxby Leics....30 E7
Saxilby Lincs....30 E3
Saxmundham Suffk....17 L2
Saxthorpe Norfk....25 H3
Scalasaig Ag & B....48 C4
Scalby N York....39 J4
Scalloway Shet....61 c6
Scarborough N York....39 K4
Scarinish Ag & B....48 b2
Scawby N Linc....34 F6
Scone P & K....51 G4
Sconser Highld....56 E6
Scotch Corner N York....38 C3
Scotter Lincs....34 F6
Scotton N York....38 B4
Scoulton Norfk....25 G5
Scourie Highld....63 G4
Scrabster Highld....65 G2
Scunthorpe N Linc....34 F5
Seaford E Susx....10 D7
Seaham Dur....43 L6
Seahouses Nthumb....47 L6
Seal Kent....10 D3
Seamer N York....39 J5
Sea Palling Norfk....25 L3
Seascale Cumb....36 D3
Seathwaite Cumb....36 F4
Seaton Devon....6 F3
Seaton Delaval Nthumb....43 K4
Seave Green N York....38 F4
Seaview IoW....9 G6
Sedbergh Cumb....37 J4
Sedgeberrow Worcs....22 B6
Sedgebrook Lincs....30 E6
Sedgefield Dur....38 D1
Sedlescombe E Susx....10 F6
Seend Wilts....13 K5
Selborne Hants....9 G3
Selby N York....34 D4
Selkirk Border....46 E6
Sellindge Kent....11 J4
Selsey W Susx....9 H6
Selston Notts....29 L4
Send Surrey....15 G7
Sennen Cnwll....2 A7
Sennybridge Powys....20 D7
Setchey Norfk....24 B7

Settle N York....37 L6
Sevenoaks Kent....10 D3
Seven Sisters Neath....19 L5
Shaftesbury Dorset....13 J8
Shalford Essex....16 F4
Shalford Surrey....9 K2
Shandon Ag & B....49 K5
Shanklin IoW....8 F7
Shap Cumb....37 H2
Shardlow Derbys....29 L6
Sharnbrook Bed....23 K4
Sharpness Gloucs....13 G2
Shaugh Prior Devon....3 L4
Shavington Ches E....28 E5
Shawbury Shrops....28 C7
Shebbear Devon....4 D6
Sheepwash Devon....4 D6
Sheerness Kent....11 G2
Sheffield Sheff....29 K2
Shefford C Beds....23 L6
Shepreth Cambs....16 C3
Shepshed Leics....30 B7
Shepton Mallet Somset....13 G6
Sherborne Dorset....7 J1
Sherburn N York....39 J5
Sherburn in Elmet N York....34 C4
Sherfield on Loddon Hants....14 D7
Sheriff Hutton N York....38 F6
Sheringham Norfk....25 H2
Shiel Bridge Highld....57 J7
Shieldaig Highld....57 H4
Shifnal Shrops....28 E8
Shildon Dur....38 C2
Shillingford Oxon....14 D4
Shillingstone Dorset....7 L2
Shinfield Wokham....14 E6
Shinness Highld....63 K6
Shipdham Norfk....25 G5
Shiplake Oxon....14 E6
Shipley C Brad....23 K3
Shipston-on-Stour Warwks....22 D6
Shipton N York....38 E7
Shiptonthorpe E R Yk....34 E3
Shirebrook Derbys....30 B3
Shoeburyness Sthend....17 G8
Shoreham-by-Sea W Susx....9 L5
Shorwell IoW....8 E7
Shotley Suffk....17 K4
Shottisham Suffk....17 L3
Shotts N Lans....45 L2
Shrewsbury Shrops....28 C8
Shrewton Wilts....13 L6
Shrivenham Oxon....13 M3
Shurdington Gloucs....22 A7
Shute Devon....6 F3
Sibsey Lincs....31 J5
Sibson Leics....22 E1
Sidmouth Devon....6 E3
Silchester Hants....14 D7
Sileby Leics....30 C7
Silk Willoughby Lincs....31 G5
Silloth Cumb....41 L6
Silsoe C Beds....23 L6
Silverdale Lancs....37 H5
Silver End Essex....16 F5
Silverstone Nhants....23 G6
Silverton Devon....5 M6
Simonburn Nthumb....42 F4
Simonsbath Somset....5 G4
Singleton W Susx....9 J4
Sissinghurst Kent....10 F4
Sittingbourne Kent....11 G3
Sixpenny Handley Dorset....8 A4
Skegness Lincs....31 L4
Skellingthorpe Lincs....30 F3
Skelmersdale Lancs....32 D6
Skelmorlie N Ayrs....49 K6
Skelton Cumb....42 C7
Skelton R & Cl....38 F2
Skenfrith Mons....21 H7
Skerray Highld....64 C2
Skipness Ag & B....44 C3
Skipsea E R Yk....35 H2
Skipton N York....33 J2
Skirling Border....46 B6
Skirwith Cumb....42 D8
Slaidburn Lancs....32 F2
Slaley Nthumb....43 G6
Slamannan Falk....45 L1
Slapton Devon....6 B7
Sleaford Lincs....31 G5
Sledmere E R Yk....39 J6
Sleights N York....39 H3

Slingsby N York....39 G5
Slough Slough....15 G5
Smailholm Border....47 G6
Smarden Kent....11 G4
Smithfield Cumb....42 C5
Snainton N York....39 J5
Snape Suffk....17 L2
Snettisham Norfk....24 E3
Snodland Kent....10 E3
Soham Cambs....24 D7
Solihull Solhll....22 C3
Solva Pembks....18 B4
Somersham Cambs....24 B7
Somerton Somset....12 F7
Sompting W Susx....9 L5
Sonning Wokham....14 E6
Sonning Common Oxon....14 E5
Sorbie D & G....40 E6
Soulby Cumb....37 K3
Souldern Oxon....22 F6
Souldrop Bed....23 K4
Sourton Devon....3 L2
Southam Warwks....22 E4
Southampton C Sotn....8 E5
South Benfleet Essex....16 F8
Southborough Kent....10 D4
South Brent Devon....6 A5
South Cave E R Yk....34 F4
South Elmsall Wakefd....34 B5
Southend Ag & B....44 B7
Southend-on-Sea Sthend....17 G8
Southery Norfk....24 D6
South Harting W Susx....9 H4
South Hayling Hants....9 G5
South Holmwood Surrey....9 L2
South Kyme Lincs....31 H5
South Mimms Herts....15 J4
Southminster Essex....17 H7
South Molton Devon....4 F5
Southmoor Oxon....14 B4
South Normanton Derbys....29 L4
South Ockendon Thurr....16 E8
South Petherton Somset....7 G1
Southport Sefton....32 C5
South Queensferry C Edin....46 B3
South Raynham Norfk....24 F4
Southrepps Norfk....25 J3
Southsea C Port....9 G6
South Shields S Tyne....43 L5
South Stainley N York....38 C6
South Walsham Norfk....25 K4
Southwell Notts....30 D4
Southwick Hants....9 G5
Southwick W Susx....10 B7
South Witham Lincs....30 F7
Southwold Suffk....25 L7
South Woodham Ferrers Essex....16 F7
South Zeal Devon....3 M2
Sowerby N York....38 D5
Sowerby Bridge Calder....33 J4
Spalding Lincs....31 H7
Sparkford Somset....13 G8
Sparsholt Hants....8 E3
Spean Bridge Highld....53 J3
Spennymoor Dur....43 K7
Spetisbury Dorset....7 L2
Spey Bay Moray....60 B3
Spilsby Lincs....31 K3
Spinningdale Highld....58 F1
Spittal Highld....65 H3
Spittal of Glenshee P & K....54 E7
Spixworth Norfk....25 J4
Spofforth N York....34 B3
Springholm D & G....41 H5
Sproatley E R Yk....35 H4
Stadhampton Oxon....14 D4
Stadhlaigearraidh W Isls....62 c11
Staffin Highld....56 E3
Stafford Staffs....28 F7
Staindrop Dur....38 B2
Staines-upon-Thames Surrey....15 G6
Stainforth N York....37 L6
Staithes N York....39 G2
Stalham Norfk....25 K4
Stamford Lincs....31 G8

Stamford Bridge E R Yk....39 G7
Stamfordham Nthumb....43 H5
Standingstone Cumb....41 K7
Standish Wigan....32 E5
Standon Herts....16 C5
Stanford in the Vale Oxon....14 B4
Stanford le Hope Thurr....10 E1
Stanhope Dur....43 G7
Stanley Dur....43 J6
Stanley P & K....50 F4
Stannington Nthumb....43 J4
Stansted Mountfitchet Essex....16 D5
Stanton Suffk....25 G7
Stanton St Quintin Wilts....13 J4
Stanway Gloucs....22 B6
Staple Fitzpaine Somset....6 F1
Stapleford Notts....30 B6
Staplehurst Kent....10 F4
Starbotton N York....37 M5
Staveley Cumb....37 H4
Staveley Derbys....29 L3
Staverton Nhants....22 F4
Staxton N York....39 J5
Steeple Essex....17 G6
Steeple Aston Oxon....22 F7
Steeple Bumpstead Essex....16 E3
Stenhousemuir Falk....50 D8
Steornabhagh W Isls....62 h3
Stevenage Herts....16 B5
Stevenston N Ayrs....44 F4
Steventon Oxon....14 C5
Stewarton E Ayrs....45 H3
Stewkley Bucks....23 J7
Steyning W Susx....9 L5
Stibb Cross Devon....4 D5
Stickford Lincs....31 J4
Stickney Lincs....31 J4
Stiffkey Norfk....25 G2
Stilligarry W Isls....62 c11
Stillington N York....38 F6
Stilton Cambs....23 L2
Stirling Stirlg....50 D7
Stock Essex....16 E7
Stockbridge Hants....8 D3
Stockport Stockp....33 H7
Stocksbridge Sheff....33 L6
Stockton-on-Tees S on T....38 E2
Stogursey Somset....12 C6
Stoke by Clare Suffk....16 F3
Stoke-by-Nayland Suffk....17 H4
Stoke Canon Devon....6 C3
Stoke Ferry Norfk....24 E5
Stoke Fleming Devon....6 C6
Stoke Gabriel Devon....6 C6
Stoke Goldington M Keyn....23 J5
Stoke Lacy Herefs....21 K5
Stoke Mandeville Bucks....14 F3
Stokenchurch Bucks....14 E4
Stoke-on-Trent C Stke....28 F5
Stoke Poges Bucks....15 G5
Stokesley N York....38 E3
Stone Staffs....28 F6
Stonehaven Abers....55 L5
Stonehouse Gloucs....13 H2
Stonehouse S Lans....45 K3
Stoneykirk D & G....40 B6
Stonor Oxon....14 E5
Stony Stratford M Keyn....23 H6
Stornoway W Isls....62 h3
Storrington W Susx....9 K4
Stotfold C Beds....16 A4
Stoulton Worcs....22 A5
Stourbridge Dudley....21 M3
Stourpaine Dorset....7 L2
Stourport-on-Severn Worcs....21 L3
Stourton Staffs....21 M2
Stow Border....46 E5
Stow-cum-Quy Cambs....16 D2
Stowmarket Suffk....17 H2
Stow-on-the-Wold Gloucs....22 C7
Strachan Abers....55 K5
Strachur Ag & B....49 J3
Stradbroke Suffk....25 J4

Stradishall Suffk 16 F3
Stradsett Norfk 24 D5
Straiton S Ayrs 45 G7
Stranraer D & G 40 B5
Stratfield Turgis
  Hants 14 E7
Stratford Gt Lon 16 C8
Stratford St Andrew
  Suffk 17 L2
Stratford-upon-
  Avon Warwks 22 C5
Strathaven S Lans 45 K4
Strathblane Stirlg 50 B8
Strathcanaird
  Highld 63 G7
Strathdon Abers 55 G3
Strathpeffer Highld 58 D4
Strathy Highld 64 E2
Strathyre Stirlg 50 B5
Stratton Cnwll 4 B6
Stratton-on-the-
  Fosse Somset 13 G6
Streatley W Berk 14 D5
Street Somset 12 F7
Strensall C York 38 F7
Strete Devon 6 C6
Stretford Traffd 33 G7
Stretham Cambs 24 C7
Stretton Rutlnd 30 F7
Strichen Abers 61 G4
Stromeferry Highld 57 H5
Stromness Ork 65 b4
Stronachlachar
  Stirlg 49 M3
Strone Ag & B 49 K5
Strontian Highld 52 F5
Strood Medway 10 F2
Stroud Gloucs 13 J2
Struy Highld 58 C5
Stuartfield Abers 61 G5
Studland Dorset 8 B7
Studley Warwks 22 B4
Sturminster Newton
  Dorset 7 K1
Sturry Kent 11 J3
Sturton by Stow
  Lincs 30 E2
Sudbury Derbys 29 H6
Sudbury Suffk 17 G3
Sulby IoM 36 c2
Summercourt Cnwll 2 E5
Sunbury-on-Thames
  Surrey 15 H6
Sunderland Sundld 43 L6
Surfleet Lincs 31 H6
Sutterton Lincs 31 J6
Sutton Cambs 24 C7
Sutton Gt Lon 10 B2
Sutton Benger Wilts 13 K4
Sutton Bridge Lincs 24 C4
Sutton Coldfield
  Birm 22 C2
Sutton Courtenay
  Oxon 14 C4
Sutton on Sea Lincs 31 L2
Sutton-on-the-
  Forest N York 38 F6
Sutton on Trent
  Notts 30 E3
Sutton Scotney
  Hants 8 E2
Sutton Valence
  Kent 10 F4
Swadlincote Derbys 29 K7
Swaffham Norfk 24 F5
Swainswick BaNES 13 H4
Swalcliffe Oxon 22 E6
Swallow Lincs 35 H6
Swallowfield
  Wokham 14 E7
Swanage Dorset 8 B7
Swanley Kent 10 D2
Swansea Swans 19 J6
Swanwick Derbys 29 K4
Swanwick Hants 8 F5
Swaton Lincs 31 G6
Swavesey Cambs 16 C1
Sway Hants 8 D6
Swindon Swindn 13 L3
Swineshead Bed 23 K4
Swineshead Lincs 31 H5
Swinford Leics 22 F3
Swinton Border 47 H5
Swinton Rothm 34 B6
Syderstone Norfk 24 F3
Symbister Shet 61 d4
Symington S Ayrs 45 G5
Symington S Lans 46 A4
Symonds Yat Herefs 21 J8
Syresham Nhants 23 G6
Syston Leics 30 C8

T

Tadcaster N York 34 B3
Tadley Hants 14 D7
Tain Highld 59 G2
Tairbeart W Isls 62 f6
Talgarreg Cerdgn 19 G2
Talgarth Powys 20 F6
Talladale Highld 57 J3
Talley Carmth 19 J3
Talmine Highld 64 C2
Talsarnau Gwynd 26 E6
Tal-y-bont Cerdgn 20 B2
Tal-y-bont Conwy 26 F3
Tal-y-bont Gwynd 26 E7
Tal-y-Cafn Conwy 27 G3
Tamworth Staffs 22 C1
Tannadice Angus 51 J2
Tan-y-groes Cerdgn 18 F2
Taplow Bucks 14 F5
Tarbert Ag & B 49 G6
Tarbert W Isls 62 f6
Tarbet Ag & B 49 L3
Tarbolton S Ayrs 45 H5
Tarland Abers 55 H4
Tarleton Lancs 32 D5
Tarporley Ches W 28 C4
Tarrant Hinton
  Dorset 7 M2
Tarskavaig Highld 56 F7
Tarves Abers 60 F6
Tarvin Ches W 28 C3
Tattershall Lincs 31 H4
Taunton Somset 12 D8
Taverham Norfk 25 H4
Tavistock Devon 3 K4
Tayinloan Ag & B 44 B3
Taynton Oxon 22 D8
Taynuilt Ag & B 53 G7
Tayport Fife 51 J4
Tayvallich Ag & B 48 F5
Tebay Cumb 37 J3
Tedburn St Mary
  Devon 6 B3
Teddington Gloucs 22 A6
Teignmouth Devon 6 C4
Telford Wrekin 28 E8
Temple Mdloth 46 D4
Temple Bar Cerdgn 19 H2
Templecombe
  Somset 13 H8
Temple Sowerby
  Cumb 37 J1
Tempsford C Beds 23 L5
Tenbury Wells Worcs ...21 K4
Tenby Pembks 18 E6
Tenterden Kent 11 G5
Ternhill Shrops 28 D6
Terrington St
  Clement Norfk 24 C4
Tetbury Gloucs 13 J3
Tetford Lincs 31 J3
Tetney Lincs 35 J6
Tetsworth Oxon 14 E4
Teviothead Border 42 C2
Tewkesbury Gloucs 21 M6
Teynham Kent 11 H3
Thame Oxon 14 E3
Thatcham W Berk 14 C6
Thaxted Essex 16 E4
Theale W Berk 14 D6
Theberton Suffk 17 M2
The Bungalow IoM 36 c2
Thetford Norfk 24 F7
Theydon Bois Essex 16 C7
Thirsk N York 38 D5
Thornbury S Glos 13 G3
Thorne Donc 34 D5
Thorney C Pete 24 A5
Thornham Norfk 24 E2
Thornhill D & G 41 J3
Thornhill Stirlg 50 C6
Thornley Dur 43 L7
Thornton Fife 51 H6
Thornton-le-Dale
  N York 39 H5
Thornton-le-Street
  N York 38 D5
Thornton Watlass
  N York 38 C5
Thorpe End Norfk 25 J3
Thorpe-le-Soken
  Essex 17 J5
Thorpeness Suffk 17 M2
Thorrington Essex 17 J5
Thrapston Nhants 23 K3
Three Cocks Powys 20 F6
Threekingham Lincs 31 G6
Threlkeld Cumb 36 F2
Threshfield N York 37 M6

Thropton Nthumb 43 H2
Thrumster Highld 65 J4
Thurcroft Rothm 34 C7
Thurlestone Devon 6 A7
Thurnscoe Barns 34 B6
Thursby Cumb 42 B6
Thurso Highld 65 G2
Thurstaston Wirral 27 K2
Thurston Suffk 17 G2
Thwaite N York 37 L4
Tibshelf Derbys 29 L4
Ticehurst E Susx 10 E5
Tickhill Donc 34 C7
Ticknall Derbys 29 K7
Tideswell Derbys 29 H3
Tidworth Wilts 8 C2
Tigh a Ghearraidh
  W Isls 62 c8
Tigharry W Isls 62 c8
Tilbury Thurr 10 E2
Tilford Surrey 9 J2
Tillicoultry Clacks 50 E6
Tilshead Wilts 13 K6
Tilstock Shrops 28 C6
Tilton on the Hill
  Leics 30 D8
Tintagel Cnwll 3 G3
Tintern Parva Mons 12 F2
Tiptree Essex 17 G5
Tisbury Wilts 13 K7
Tissington Derbys 29 J5
Tittensor Staffs 28 F6
Tiverton Devon 5 H6
Tobermory Ag & B 52 C5
Toddington C Beds 23 K7
Todmorden Calder 33 H4
Toft Shet 61 c3
Toft Hill Dur 38 B1
Tolastadh W Isls 62 i2
Tollard Royal Wilts 7 M1
Tollesbury Essex 17 H6
Tolleshunt D'Arcy
  Essex 17 G6
Tolpuddle Dorset 7 K3
Tolsta W Isls 62 i2
Tomatin Highld 59 G6
Tomintoul Moray 54 F3
Tomnavoulin Moray 59 K6
Tonbridge Kent 10 E4
Tongue Highld 64 C3
Tonypandy Rhondd 12 B3
Tonyrefail Rhondd 12 B3
Topcliffe N York 38 D5
Topsham Devon 6 D3
Torbeg N Ayrs 44 C5
Torcross Devon 6 B7
Tore Highld 58 E4
Torksey Lincs 30 E3
Torphichen W Loth 46 A3
Torphins Abers 55 J4
Torpoint Cnwll 3 K5
Torquay Torbay 6 C5
Torrance E Duns 45 J1
Torridon Highld 57 H4
Torrin Highld 56 F7
Torryburn Fife 46 B2
Torthorwald D & G 41 K4
Torver Cumb 36 F4
Totland IoW 8 D6
Totnes Devon 6 B5
Totton Hants 8 D4
Towcester Nhants 23 G5
Tow Law Dur 43 J7
Town Yetholm
  Border 47 H6
Traquair Border 46 D6
Trawden Lancs 33 H3
Trawsfynydd Gwynd 26 F6
Trearddur Bay IoA 26 B2
Trecastle Powys 20 D7
Tredegar Blae G 12 C1
Treen Cnwll 2 A8
Trefriw Conwy 27 G4
Tregaron Cerdgn 19 J1
Tregony Cnwll 2 F6
Treherbert Rhondd 19 M6
Trellech Mons 12 F2
Tremadog Gwynd 26 E5
Trimdon Dur 43 L7
Trimingham Norfk 25 J3
Tring Herts 14 F3
Trinity Jersey 7 b1
Troon S Ayrs 45 G5
Trotton W Susx 9 J5
Troutbeck Cumb 37 G3
Trowbridge Wilts 13 J5
Truro Cnwll 2 E6
Tugby Leics 23 H1
Tullibody Clacks 50 D7
Tummel Bridge P & K ...50 D2
Tunbridge Wells Kent ..10 E4

Tunstall Suffk 17 L2
Turnberry S Ayrs 44 F7
Turnditch Derbys 29 K5
Turner's Hill W Susx 10 B5
Turriff Abers 60 E4
Turvey Bed 23 K5
Tutbury Staffs 29 J6
Tuxford Notts 30 D3
Twycross Leics 22 E1
Twyford Hants 8 E4
Twyford Wokham 14 E6
Twynholm D & G 41 G6
Tyndrum Stirlg 53 K7
Tynemouth N Tyne 43 L5
Tytherleigh Devon 6 F2
Tywyn Gwynd 20 A1

U

Uckfield E Susx 10 D6
Uffculme Devon 5 J6
Uffington Oxon 14 A5
Ugborough Devon 6 A6
Uig Highld 56 D3
Ulceby N Linc 35 H5
Uldale Cumb 42 A7
Ullapool Highld 63 G7
Ullenhall Warwks 22 C4
Ulpha Cumb 36 E4
Ulsta Shet 61 c3
Ulverston Cumb 36 F5
Umberleigh Devon 4 F5
Unapool Highld 63 H4
Upavon Wilts 13 L5
Uplyme Devon 6 F3
Upottery Devon 6 E2
Upper Beeding
  W Susx 9 L5
Upper Benefield
  Nhants 23 K2
Upper Broughton
  Notts 30 D7
Upper Largo Fife 51 J6
Upper Lydbrook
  Gloucs 21 K8
Upper Tean Staffs 29 G5
Uppingham Rutlnd 23 J1
Upstreet Kent 11 K3
Upton Snodsbury
  Worcs 22 A5
Upton-upon-Severn
  Worcs 21 M6
Urchfont Wilts 13 K5
Usk Mons 12 E2
Uttoxeter Staffs 29 H6
Uxbridge Gt Lon 15 H5
Uyeasound Shet 61 d2

V

Vale Guern 6 b1
Ventnor IoW 8 F7
Verwood Dorset 8 B5
Vidlin Shet 61 c4
Virginia Water
  Surrey 15 G6
Voe Shet 61 c4

W

Waddesdon Bucks 14 E3
Waddington Lancs 33 G3
Waddington Lincs 30 F4
Wadebridge Cnwll 2 F4
Wadesmill Herts 15 K3
Wadhurst E Susx 10 E5
Wainfleet All Saints
  Lincs 31 K4
Wakefield Wakefd 33 M5
Walberswick Suffk 25 L7
Walgherton Ches E 28 E5
Walkerburn Border 46 D6
Walkern Herts 16 B5
Walkington E R Yk 35 G3
Wallasey Wirral 32 C7
Wallingford Oxon 14 D5
Walls Shet 61 b5
Walsall Wsall 22 B1
Waltham NE Lin 35 J6
Waltham Abbey
  Essex 16 C7
Waltham on the
  Wolds Leics 30 E7
Walton Powys 21 G4
Walton Somset 12 F7

Walton-on-Thames
Surrey 15 H6
Walton on the Naze
Essex 17 K5
Wanlockhead D & G.... 45 L6
Wansford C Pete 23 L1
Wanstrow Somset 13 H6
Wantage Oxon 14 B5
Warboys Cambs 24 A7
Warcop Cumb............ 37 K2
Wardlow Derbys......... 29 J3
Ware Herts 15 K3
Wareham Dorset........... 7 L3
Warenford Nthumb.... 47 L6
Wargrave Wokham 14 E6
Wark Nthumb............ 42 F4
Wark Nthumb............ 47 H6
Warkworth Nthumb.... 43 K2
Warmington
Warwks 22 E5
Warminster Wilts 13 J6
Warninglid W Susx 10 B5
Warrington Warrtn ... 32 F7
Warsash Hants 8 E5
Warslow Staffs 29 H4
Warton Lancs 32 D4
Warwick Warwks 22 D4
Wasbister Ork 65 b2
Wasdale Head Cumb.. 36 E3
Washingborough
Lincs 30 F3
Washington Sundld.... 43 K6
Watchet Somset........... 5 J3
Watchgate Cumb........ 37 H4
Waterbeach Cambs.... 16 D2
Waterbeck D & G....... 42 A4
Waterhouses Staffs... 29 H5
Waterlooville Hants..... 9 G5
Watermillock Cumb.... 37 G2
Watford Herts........... 15 H4
Watford Nhants......... 23 G4
Wath upon Dearne
Rothm 34 B6
Watlington Oxon....... 14 E4
Watten Highld........... 65 H3
Watton Norfk 24 F5
Watton-at-Stone
Herts 15 K2
Wearhead Dur.......... 42 F7
Weasenham All
Saints Norfk 24 F4
Weaverham Ches W ... 28 D3
Wedmore Somset 12 E6
Weedon Nhants......... 23 G4
Week St Mary Cnwll..... 4 B7
Weem P & K.............. 50 D2
Welbourn Lincs......... 30 F4
Wellesbourne
Warwks 22 D5
Wellingborough
Nhants 23 J4
Wellington Somset 5 K5
Wellington Wrekin 28 D8
Wells Somset............ 12 F6
Wells-next-the-sea
Norfk 24 F2
Welney Norfk 24 C6
Welshampton Shrops.. 28 B6
Welshpool Powys...... 27 K8
Welton Nhants.......... 23 G4
Welwyn Herts........... 15 J3
Welwyn Garden City
Herts 15 J3
Wem Shrops 28 C6
Wembley Gt Lon....... 15 J5
Wembury Devon 3 L6
Wendover Bucks....... 14 F3
Wensley N York......... 38 B4
Wentbridge Wakefd.. 34 B5
Weobley Herefs........ 21 H5
Wereham Norfk......... 24 D5
West Auckland Dur.... 38 B2
West Bay Dorset......... 7 H3
West Bexington
Dorset 7 H3
West Bilney Norfk..... 24 E4
West Bridgford
Notts........................ 30 C6
West Bromwich
Sandw 22 B2
Westbury Shrops....... 28 B8
Westbury Wilts......... 13 J6
West Calder W Loth... 46 A4
West Chiltington
W Susx 9 K4
Westcott Surrey 9 L2
Westerham Kent....... 10 C3
West Felton Shrops... 27 L7
Westfield E Susx....... 10 F6
West Haddon Nhants.. 23 G3
West Hoathly W Susx.. 10 C5

West Horsley Surrey 15 H8
West Huntspill
Somset 12 D6
West Kilbride N Ayrs.. 44 F3
West Kirby Wirral....... 27 K7
West Lavington Wilts.. 13 K6
West Linton Border.... 46 C5
West Lulworth
Dorset........................ 7 L4
West Lynn Norfk....... 24 D4
West Malvern Worcs... 21 L5
West Meon Hants......... 9 G4
West Mersea Essex.... 17 H6
West Moors Dorset...... 8 B5
Westnewton Cumb.... 41 L7
West Newton Norfk... 24 E3
Weston Herts 8 A4
Weston Staffs........... 29 G6
Westonbirt Gloucs.... 13 J3
Weston Heath
Shrops 28 E7
Weston-on-the-
Green Oxon 14 C3
Weston-sub-Edge
Gloucs 22 C6
Weston-super-Mare
N Som 12 D5
Weston-under-
Redcastle Shrops.... 28 D6
West Pennard
Somset 12 F7
West Pentire Cnwll...... 2 F7
West Rounton N York.. 38 D3
West Runton Norfk.... 25 J2
Westruther Border.... 47 G5
West Sandwick Shet.. 61 d3
Westward Ho! Devon.... 4 D4
West Wittering
W Susx 9 H6
West Witton N York... 38 A4
West Woodburn
Nthumb..................... 43 G3
Wetheral Cumb......... 42 C6
Wetherby Leeds........ 34 B3
Wetwang E R Yk........ 39 J7
Weybourne Norfk..... 25 H2
Weybridge Surrey..... 15 H7
Weyhill Hants............. 8 D2
Weymouth Dorset....... 7 J4
Whaley Bridge
Derbys 29 G2
Whalley Lancs 33 G3
Whaplode Lincs 31 J7
Whaplode Drove
Lincs 31 J7
Whauphill D & G........ 40 E6
Wheathampstead
Herts 15 J3
Wheatley Oxon......... 14 D3
Wheddon Cross
Somset 5 H4
Whepstead Suffk...... 17 G2
Wherwell Hants........... 8 E2
Whickham Gatesd..... 43 J5
Whiddon Down
Devon 6 A3
Whimple Devon.......... 6 D3
Whipsnade C Beds..... 15 G3
Whitburn W Loth....... 46 A4
Whitby N York 39 H3
Whitchurch Bucks.... 14 E2
Whitchurch Hants....... 8 E2
Whitchurch Herefs... 21 J8
Whitchurch Shrops... 28 C8
Whitebridge Highld... 58 D7
Whitehaven Cumb..... 36 D2
Whitehill and
Bordon Hants 9 H3
Whitehills Abers....... 60 D3
Whitehouse Ag & B... 49 G6
Whitekirk E Loth....... 46 F2
Whitewell Lancs....... 32 F3
Whithorn D & G........ 40 E7
Whiting Bay N Ayrs... 44 E5
Whitland Carmth...... 18 E5
Whitley Bay N Tyne... 43 K5
Whitley Chapel
Nthumb..................... 43 G6
Whitminster Gloucs... 13 H1
Whitstable Kent....... 11 J2
Whittington Shrops... 27 L6
Whittlebury Nhants... 23 G6
Whittlesey Cambs..... 24 A6
Whitton Powys......... 21 G4
Whitwell Derbys....... 30 B3
Whitwell Herts 15 J3
Wick Highld.............. 65 J3
Wickford Essex......... 16 F7
Wickham Hants........... 8 F5
Wickham Market
Suffk 17 K2

Wickwar S Glos.......... 13 H3
Widdrington
Nthumb..................... 43 K3
Widecombe in the
Moor Devon.............. 6 A4
Widegates Cnwll......... 3 J5
Widemouth Bay
Cnwll 4 B6
Widford Herts 16 C5
Widmerpool Notts.... 30 C6
Widnes Halton.......... 28 C2
Wigan Wigan............ 32 E6
Wiggenhall St
Germans Norfk...... 24 D4
Wigston Leics........... 23 G1
Wigton Cumb............ 42 A6
Wigtown D & G......... 40 E6
Wilberfoss E R Yk..... 34 D2
Wilby Nhants............ 23 J4
Willand Devon............ 5 J6
Willingham Cambs.... 24 B8
Wilmcote Warwks..... 22 C4
Wilmington Devon....... 6 F2
Wilmslow Ches E...... 28 F2
Wilsontown S Lans... 46 A4
Wilstead Bed............ 23 J5
Wilton Wilts 13 L7
Wimbledon Gt Lon... 15 J6
Wimblington Cambs.. 24 B6
Wimborne Minster
Dorset........................ 8 A5
Wincanton Somset.... 13 H7
Winchcombe Gloucs... 22 B7
Winchelsea E Susx.... 11 G6
Winchester Hants....... 8 E3
Windermere Cumb.... 37 G4
Windsor W & M.......... 15 G6
Wing Bucks............... 14 F2
Wingate Dur............. 43 L7
Wingham Kent.......... 11 K3
Winkfield Br For........ 14 F6
Winkleigh Devon......... 4 F6
Winscombe N Som.... 12 E5
Winsford Ches W...... 28 D3
Winsford Somset........ 5 H4
Winsham Somset........ 7 G2
Winslow Bucks......... 23 H7
Winster Derbys......... 29 J4
Winterborne
Monkton Dorset....... 7 J3
Winterborne
Stickland Dorset....... 7 L2
Winterborne
Whitechurch
Dorset........................ 7 L2
Winterbourne
Abbas Dorset............ 7 J3
Winterbourne Stoke
Wilts......................... 13 L7
Winteringham
N Linc 34 F5
Winterslow Wilts........ 8 C3
Winterton N Linc....... 34 F5
Winwick Cambs........ 23 L3
Wirksworth Derbys... 29 J4
Wisbech Cambs........ 31 K8
Wisborough Green
W Susx 9 K3
Wishaw N Lans......... 45 L3
Witham Essex........... 16 F5
Witheridge Devon....... 5 G6
Withern Lincs........... 31 K2
Withernsea E R Yk.... 35 K4
Withington Gloucs... 22 B8
Withington Herefs... 21 J8
Withyham E Susx..... 10 D5
Withypool Somset...... 5 H4
Witnesham Suffk..... 17 J3
Witney Oxon 14 B3
Wittersham Kent..... 11 G5
Witton le Wear Dur... 43 J8
Wiveliscombe
Somset 5 J4
Wivelsfield E Susx... 10 C6
Wivenhoe Essex....... 17 H5
Wix Essex................. 17 J4
Woburn C Beds........ 23 K6
Woking Surrey.......... 15 G7
Wokingham Wokham.. 14 F6
Wolf's Castle
Pembks 18 C4
Wollaston Nhants..... 23 J4
Wollaston Shrops..... 27 L8
Wolsingham Dur...... 43 H7
Wolverhampton
Wolves 21 M1
Wolvey Warwks........ 22 E2
Wolviston S on T...... 38 E2
Wombourne Staffs... 21 M2
Wombwell Barns..... 34 B6
Wooburn Bucks....... 14 F5

Woodbridge Suffk..... 17 K3
Woodchurch Kent..... 11 G5
Woodford Gloucs..... 13 G2
Woodhall Spa Lincs.. 31 H4
Woodland Dur.......... 38 B2
Woodstock Oxon..... 14 C3
Woofferton Shrops... 21 J4
Wookey Hole Somset.. 12 F6
Wool Dorset.............. 7 L3
Woolacombe Devon.... 4 D3
Wooler Nthumb........ 47 K6
Woolhampton
W Berk...................... 14 D6
Woolpit Suffk........... 17 H2
Woolwich Gt Lon..... 10 C1
Woore Shrops........... 28 E5
Wootton N Linc........ 35 G5
Wootton Oxon.......... 14 B2
Wootton Bassett
Wilts......................... 13 L3
Wootton Courtenay
Somset 5 H3
Wootton Wawen
Warwks 22 C4
Worcester Worcs...... 21 M5
Workington Cumb..... 36 D1
Worksop Notts......... 30 C2
Worlingworth Suffk... 17 K1
Wormit Fife.............. 51 J4
Worplesdon Surrey... 15 G7
Worthen Shrops....... 21 G1
Worthing W Susx........ 9 L5
Worth Matravers
Dorset........................ 7 M4
Wotton-under-Edge
Gloucs 13 H3
Wragby Lincs........... 31 G3
Wrangaton Devon....... 6 A6
Wrangle Lincs........... 31 K5
Wrawby N Linc......... 35 G6
Wrelton N York........ 39 G5
Wrentham Suffk....... 25 L7
Wrestlingworth
C Beds...................... 16 B3
Wrexham Wrexhm.... 27 L5
Wroughton Swindn... 13 L4
Wroxall IoW............... 8 F7
Wroxeter Shrops...... 28 D8
Wroxham Norfk........ 25 K4
Wroxton Oxon.......... 22 E6
Wyboston Bed.......... 23 L5
Wye Kent.................. 11 H4
Wylye Wilts.............. 13 K7
Wymondham Leics... 30 E7
Wymondham Norfk... 25 H5

Y

Yarcombe Devon........... 6 F2
Yardley Gobion
Nhants 23 H5
Yardley Hastings
Nhants 23 J5
Yarm S on T.............. 38 D3
Yarmouth IoW............ 8 D6
Yarrowford Border.... 46 E6
Yateley Hants........... 14 F7
Yatton S Som............ 12 E5
Yatton Keynell Wilts.. 13 J4
Yaxley Cambs........... 23 M2
Yeadon Leeds........... 33 K3
Yealmpton Devon....... 3 L5
Yelverton Devon......... 3 L4
Yelverton Norfk........ 25 K5
Yeovil Somset............ 7 H1
Yeovilton Somset...... 12 F8
Yetts o'Muckhart
Clacks 50 E6
Y Felinheli Gwynd.... 26 D3
Y Maerdy Conwy....... 27 J5
York C York............... 34 C2
Youlgreave Derbys.... 29 J4
Yoxall Staffs............ 29 H7
Yoxford Suffk........... 17 L1
Y Rhiw Gwynd.......... 26 B6
Ysbyty Ystwyth
Cerdgn...................... 20 B3
Ystalyfera Neath...... 19 K5
Ystradgynlais
Powys 19 K5
Ystrad Mynach
Caerph...................... 12 C2

Z

Zeals Wilts............... 13 H7
Zennor Cnwll.............. 2 B6

This chart shows distances in miles between two towns along AA-recommended routes. Using motorways and other main roads this is normally the fastest route, though not necessarily the shortest.

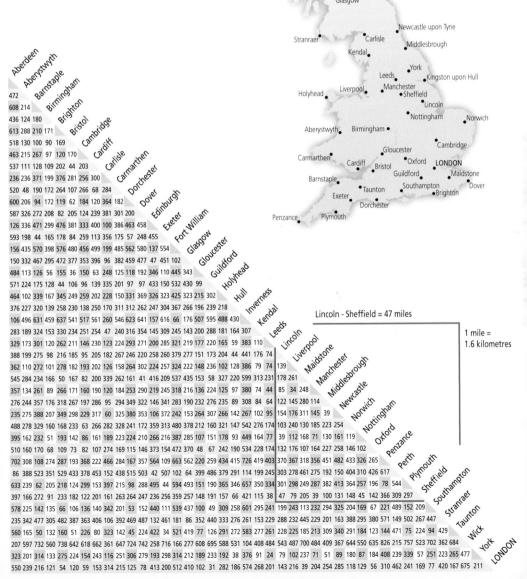

Aberdeen
Aberystwyth
Barnstaple
Birmingham
Brighton
Bristol
Cambridge
Cardiff
Carlisle
Carmarthen
Dorchester
Dover
Edinburgh
Exeter
Fort William
Glasgow
Gloucester
Guildford
Holyhead
Hull
Inverness
Kendal
Leeds
Lincoln
Liverpool
Maidstone
Manchester
Middlesbrough
Newcastle
Norwich
Nottingham
Oxford
Penzance
Perth
Plymouth
Sheffield
Southampton
Stranraer
Taunton
Wick
York
LONDON

```
472
608 214
436 124 180
613 288 210 171
518 130 100 90 169
463 215 267 97 120 170
537 111 128 109 202 44 203
236 236 371 199 376 281 256 300
520 48 190 172 264 107 266 68 284
600 206 94 172 119 62 184 120 364 182
587 326 272 208 82 205 124 239 381 301 200
126 336 471 299 476 381 333 400 100 386 463 458
593 198 44 165 178 84 259 113 356 175 57 248 455
156 435 570 398 576 480 456 499 199 485 562 580 137 554
150 332 467 295 472 377 353 396 96 382 459 477 47 451 102
484 113 126 56 155 36 150 63 248 125 118 192 346 110 445 343
571 224 175 128 44 106 96 139 335 201 97 97 433 150 532 430 99
464 102 339 167 345 249 259 202 228 150 331 369 326 323 425 323 215 302
376 227 320 139 258 230 138 250 170 311 312 262 247 304 367 266 196 239 218
106 496 631 459 637 541 517 561 260 546 623 641 157 616 66 176 507 595 488 430
283 189 324 153 330 234 251 254 47 240 316 354 145 309 245 143 200 288 181 164 307
329 173 301 120 262 211 146 230 123 224 293 271 200 285 321 219 177 220 165 59 383 110
388 199 275 98 216 185 95 205 182 267 246 220 258 260 379 277 151 173 204 44 441 176 74
362 110 272 101 278 182 193 202 126 158 264 302 224 257 324 222 148 236 102 128 386 79 74 139
545 284 234 166 50 167 82 200 339 262 161 41 416 209 537 435 153 58 327 220 599 313 231 178 261
357 134 261 89 266 171 160 190 120 184 253 290 219 245 318 216 136 224 125 97 380 74 44 85 34 248
276 244 357 176 318 267 197 286 95 294 349 322 146 341 283 190 232 276 235 89 308 84 64 122 145 280 114
235 275 388 207 349 298 229 317 60 325 380 353 106 372 242 153 264 307 266 142 267 102 95 154 176 311 145 39
488 278 329 160 168 233 63 266 282 328 241 172 359 313 480 378 212 160 321 147 542 276 174 103 240 130 185 223 254
395 162 232 51 193 142 36 161 189 223 224 210 266 216 387 285 107 151 178 93 449 164 77 39 112 168 71 130 161 119
510 160 170 68 109 73 82 107 274 169 115 146 373 154 472 370 48 67 242 190 534 228 174 132 176 107 164 227 258 146 102
702 308 108 274 287 193 368 222 466 284 167 357 564 109 663 562 220 259 434 415 726 419 403 370 367 318 356 451 482 433 326 265
86 388 523 351 529 433 378 453 152 438 515 503 42 507 102 64 399 486 379 291 114 199 245 303 278 461 275 192 150 404 310 426 617
633 239 62 205 218 124 299 153 397 215 98 288 495 44 594 493 151 190 365 346 657 350 334 301 298 249 287 382 413 364 257 196 78 544
397 166 272 91 233 182 122 201 161 263 264 247 236 259 359 257 148 191 157 66 421 115 38 47 79 205 39 100 131 148 45 142 366 309 297
578 225 142 135 66 106 136 140 342 201 53 152 440 111 539 437 100 49 309 258 601 295 241 199 243 113 232 294 325 204 169 67 221 489 152 209
235 342 477 305 482 387 363 406 106 392 469 487 132 461 181 86 352 440 333 276 261 153 229 288 232 445 229 201 163 388 295 380 571 149 502 267 447
560 165 50 132 160 51 226 80 323 142 45 224 422 34 521 419 77 126 291 272 583 277 261 228 225 185 213 309 340 291 184 123 144 471 75 224 94 429
207 597 732 560 738 642 618 662 361 647 724 742 258 716 166 277 608 695 588 531 104 408 484 543 487 700 484 409 367 644 550 635 826 215 757 523 702 362 684
323 201 314 133 275 224 154 243 116 251 306 279 193 298 314 212 189 233 192 38 376 91 24 79 102 237 71 51 89 180 87 184 408 239 339 57 251 223 265 477
550 239 216 121 54 120 59 153 314 215 125 78 413 200 512 410 102 31 282 186 574 268 201 143 216 39 204 254 285 118 129 56 310 462 241 169 77 420 167 675 211
```

Lincoln - Sheffield = 47 miles

1 mile = 1.6 kilometres

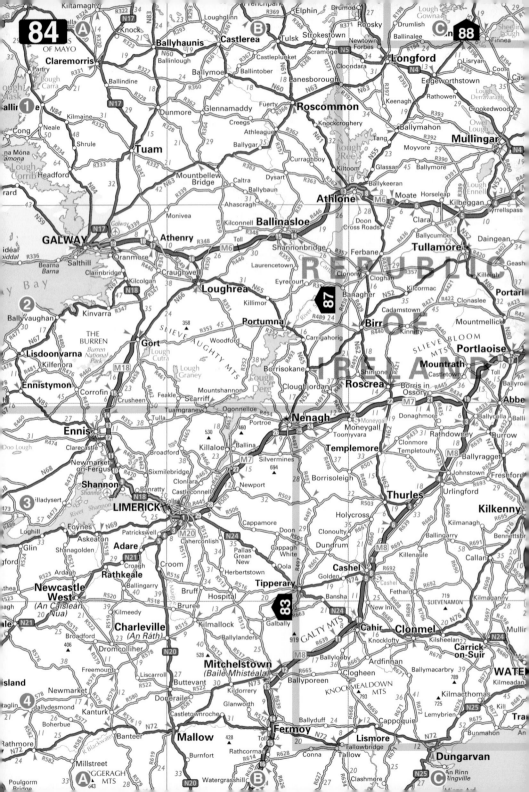

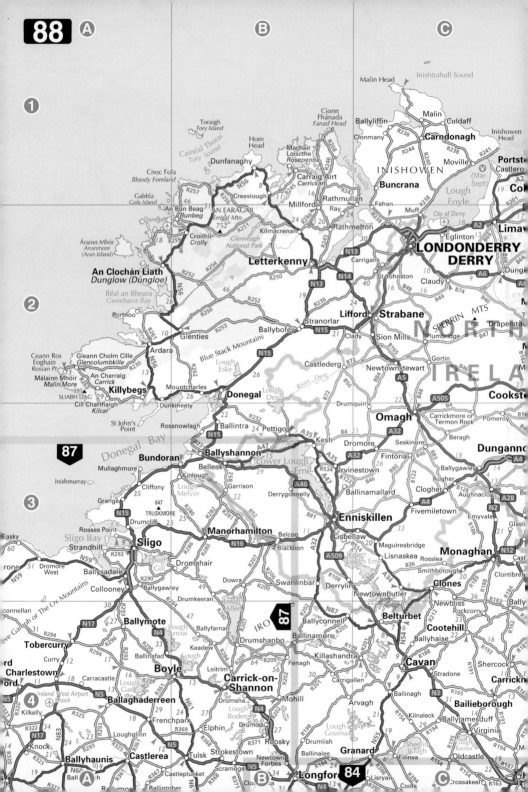

1

Rathlin
Island

White Park
Bay

Portballintrae
Bushmills
ush
Ballycastle
Dervock   Armoy
Cushendun
A29
B17
B66 B67
B15
20
A2
19
Ballymoney
Cushendall
Red Bay
B14
Garron Point
A26
A54
Aghadowey   Dunloy
Garvagh   Rasharkin
B70
Kilrea
Cullybackey
Portglenone
Gulladuff Ahoghill
Bellaghy
Carnlough
Martinstown
Glenarm
Ballymena   **Larne**
Moorfields
A36
Ballygalley
Island
Magee
Whitehead
Ballycarry
Carrickfergus
NEWTOWNABBEY
Crawfordsburn
BANGOR
Donaghadee
Holywood
A48
Newtownards
BELFAST
George Best
Dundonald
Ballywalter
Greyabbey
Kircubbin
Portavogie
Comber
Ballygowan
Saintfield
Strangford
Lough
Killyleagh
Portaferry
Strangford
Downpatrick
Clough
Ardglass
St John's Point
Newcastle
850
MOURNE
MTS
Annalong
Warrenpoint
Rostrevor
Omeath
Carlingford
Kilkeel
Greenore

Troon
(Mar-Oct)
Cairnryan
(Apr-Sept)
Douglas
Cairnryan
Liverpool
(Birkenhead)

2

3

4

Distance chart - Ireland

This chart shows distances, in both miles and kilometres, between two towns along AA-recommended routes. Using motorways and other main roads this is normally the fastest route, though not necessarily the shortest.

For example, the distance between Cork and Omagh is 435 kilometres or 270 miles (8 kilometres is approximately 5 miles).

Distances in miles

	Athlone	Belfast	Béal an Mhuirthead (Belmullet)	Cavan	Clifden	Cork	Donegal	Downpatrick	Dublin	Dundalk	An Clochán Liath (Dunglow)	Dún Laoghaire	Ennis	Enniskillen	Galway	Kilkee	Kilkenny	Killarney	Larne	Limerick	Londonderry (Derry)	Mallow	Omagh	Portlaoise	Portrush	Roscommon	Sligo	Tipperary	Tralee	Tullamore	Waterford	An Coireán (Waterville)	Wexford	Wicklow
Armagh	99	41	168	83	196	246	84	53	86	33	96	93	167	50	150	299	164	274	62	208	71	233	37	138	68	101	92	197	268	145	186	313	180	123
Athlone		148	123	95	101	136	113	144	78	93	150	89	68	84	57	189	76	142	170	74	145	115	111	45	160	20	74	89	138	28	114	182	116	111
Belfast			202	117	230	264	116	22	105	51	129	111	251	84	231	319	182	294	22	228	72	252	70	156	63	142	126	215	288	165	205	333	200	143
Béal an Mhuirthead (Belmullet)				98	91	231	116	212	189	195	153	201	144	118	111	274	199	236	223	167	161	210	144	169	199	103	76	191	232	147	236	277	239	216
Cavan					153	187	69	100	68	61	106	84	121	132	103	239	143	193	109	125	93	166	59	90	109	55	70	139	189	68	168	233	161	104
Clifden						170	144	240	177	196	181	187	91	146	50	215	179	178	251	113	189	150	172	148	227	98	104	138	171	125	189	216	218	207
Cork							248	257	157	213	285	167	87	214	122	57	92	56	286	64	304	22	270	108	308	156	208	64	76	129	80	99	112	185
Donegal								127	143	111	36	156	161	42	128	285	215	248	120	184	46	220	47	159	84	93	40	209	242	138	240	287	229	172
Downpatrick									98	44	144	104	246	95	226	314	175	289	44	223	93	245	80	155	85	146	136	214	282	160	198	327	194	138
Dublin										53	176	8	147	99	129	214	80	192	126	124	151	150	112	54	150	96	133	114	182	66	103	227	92	35
Dundalk											131	59	168	64	152	266	130	241	73	175	99	200	65	105	98	102	105	164	235	81	153	280	147	90
An Clochán Liath (Dunglow)												178	198	74	165	322	251	284	136	221	61	256	59	196	91	130	77	246	278	175	276	323	269	212
Dún Laoghaire													152	114	139	221	85	197	133	129	153	155	119	59	160	107	139	119	193	71	110	238	83	26
Ennis														153	42	130	122	92	273	23	207	66	186	91	229	86	122	47	88	101	101	133	139	174
Enniskillen															136	270	173	225	106	157	61	198	27	122	98	86	41	170	221	100	198	265	192	135
Galway																172	131	134	223	64	173	102	165	101	210	49	88	89	124	80	142	169	171	159
Kilkee																	155	63	306	57	241	97	222	125	263	127	156	82	43	137	135	96	173	208
Kilkenny																		121	200	75	224	80	189	31	228	96	150	51	139	51	30	172	65	87
Killarney																			315	70	285	42	251	136	339	162	208	92	20	137	119	50	157	216
Larne																				250	75	273	75	178	55	164	147	241	310	187	226	355	222	165
Limerick																					219	43	183	68	273	94	145	25	65	69	78	110	116	151
Londonderry (Derry)																						296	34	202	40	137	85	261	280	161	250	325	242	185
Mallow																							260	95	298	136	181	51	63	116	78	92	116	175
Omagh																								168	71	114	68	227	247	127	215	292	203	147
Portlaoise																									205	66	120	59	132	21	66	177	70	82
Portrush																										163	122	278	347	224	267	392	259	202
Roscommon																											53	109	158	44	134	203	136	129
Sligo																												169	202	98	186	247	190	159
Tipperary																													88	80	53	133	91	141
Tralee																														133	139	53	177	215
Tullamore																															87	178	91	93
Waterford																																170	38	80
An Coireán (Waterville)																																	208	256
Wexford																																		59

Distances in kilometres

	Armagh	Athlone	Belfast	Béal an Mhuirthead (Belmullet)	Cavan	Clifden	Cork	Donegal	Downpatrick	Dublin	Dundalk	An Clochán Liath (Dunglow)	Dún Laoghaire	Ennis	Enniskillen	Galway	Kilkee	Kilkenny	Killarney	Larne	Limerick	Londonderry (Derry)	Mallow	Omagh	Portlaoise	Portrush	Roscommon	Sligo	Tipperary	Tralee	Tullamore	Waterford	An Coireán (Waterville)	Wexford
Athlone	159																																	
Belfast	66	238																																
Béal an Mhuirthead (Belmullet)	270	198	324																															
Cavan	144	84	141	238																														
Clifden	315	163	370	147	246																													
Cork	396	218	425	371	300	274																												
Donegal	135	182	187	187	111	232	399																											
Downpatrick	85	232	35	342	161	387	414	204																										
Dublin	139	125	169	305	109	285	253	230	157																									
Dundalk	53	150	83	314	99	316	342	179	71	85																								
An Clochán Liath (Dunglow)	155	242	207	246	171	291	459	58	232	283	211																							
Dún Laoghaire	150	143	179	324	135	301	269	251	167	13	95	287																						
Ennis	269	110	404	232	194	146	139	260	396	236	271	319	245																					
Enniskillen	81	135	135	189	52	235	345	68	152	159	102	119	184	245																				
Galway	241	91	372	179	166	80	196	205	364	208	244	265	224	67	219																			
Kilkee	324	176	259	287	261	202	188	315	449	291	329	375	300	55	309	123																		
Kilkenny	257	122	287	321	230	288	148	346	282	123	204	404	137	196	279	211	250																	
Killarney	441	228	473	380	310	287	90	399	465	309	388	457	317	149	363	216	101	195																
Larne	100	274	36	359	175	404	460	193	71	203	117	219	214	440	170	359	493	322	507															
Limerick	335	119	367	268	201	184	103	296	359	199	282	356	208	37	252	104	92	121	112	403														
Londonderry (Derry)	114	233	115	259	149	305	490	74	150	242	159	98	246	333	98	278	388	361	481	120	353													
Mallow	376	185	405	338	268	242	35	354	394	241	322	412	250	106	319	164	156	129	67	440	69	477												
Omagh	60	178	112	232	95	277	435	75	129	180	104	95	192	300	43	266	357	304	405	120	295	55	419											
Portlaoise	222	73	251	272	145	238	173	256	250	87	168	315	95	146	197	163	202	49	219	286	110	325	153	271										
Portrush	109	258	101	319	175	365	496	135	136	242	158	147	258	369	158	338	424	367	546	89	440	64	480	115	330									
Roscommon	163	32	299	166	88	157	251	150	235	155	164	209	172	139	138	78	205	155	261	263	152	221	219	184	106	262								
Sligo	147	118	202	123	112	168	335	64	219	214	169	123	224	196	67	141	252	241	335	236	233	137	291	110	192	193	86							
Tipperary	317	143	347	308	224	223	102	336	345	183	263	396	192	76	274	144	132	82	148	388	40	420	82	366	95	447	176	272						
Tralee	432	221	464	374	303	275	122	390	454	293	378	448	311	142	355	200	69	223	33	499	105	451	99	398	212	559	254	325	141					
Tullamore	233	45	266	237	109	201	207	221	258	106	131	281	113	163	161	129	221	83	221	301	111	259	189	204	34	361	71	158	128	214				
Waterford	301	184	330	380	271	304	129	386	320	167	248	444	177	162	319	229	218	48	192	366	126	403	125	346	106	431	216	300	86	224	140			
An Coireán (Waterville)	504	294	536	446	376	348	159	462	527	366	451	520	383	214	427	272	154	277	82	572	177	523	148	470	285	631	327	398	214	85	286	273		
Wexford	290	186	322	385	260	351	180	370	312	148	237	433	134	223	310	275	278	105	253	357	186	390	187	327	113	417	219	305	147	285	147	61	334	
Wicklow	198	178	230	348	166	333	298	276	222	56	145	341	42	280	217	256	335	140	348	266	243	298	282	236	131	325	207	256	227	346	150	129	412	95

This index lists places appearing in the main-map section of the atlas in alphabetical order. The reference following each name gives the atlas page number and grid reference of the square in which the place appears. The map shows counties, unitary authorities and administrative areas, together with a list of the abbreviated name forms used in the index.

Northern Ireland

Antrim	**Antrim**
Armagh	**Armagh**
Belfst	**Belfast**
Down	**Down**
Ferman	**Fermanagh**
Lderry	**Londonderry Derry**
Tyrone	**Tyrone**

Republic of Ireland

Carlow	**Carlow**
Cavan	**Cavan**
Clare	**Clare**
Cork	**Cork**
Donegl	**Donegal**
Dublin	**Dublin**
Dublin	**Dublin City (1)**
Dublin	**Dún Laoghaire-Rathdown (2)**
Dublin	**Fingal (3)**
Dublin	**South Dublin (4)**
Galway	**Galway**
Kerry	**Kerry**
Kildre	**Kildare**
Kilken	**Kilkenny**
Laois	**Laois**
Leitrm	**Leitrim**
Limrck	**Limerick**
Longfd	**Longford**
Louth	**Louth**
Mayo	**Mayo**
Meath	**Meath**
Monhan	**Monaghan**
Offaly	**Offaly**
Roscom	**Roscommon**
Sligo	**Sligo**
Tippry	**Tipperary North**
Tippry	**Tipperary South**
Watfd	**Waterford**
Wmeath	**Westmeath**
Wexfd	**Wexford**
Wicklw	**Wicklow**

A

Abbeydorney Kerry 82 C2
Abbeyfeale Limrck 82 C2
Abbeyleix Laois 84 C3
Adamstown Wexfd 85 D4
Adare Limrck 83 D2
Adrigole Cork 82 C3
Aghadowey Lderry 89 D2
Ahascragh Galway 87 D3
Ahoghill Antrim 89 D2
Allihies Cork 82 B3
Anascaul Kerry 82 B2
An Bun Beag Donegl 88 B2
An Charraig Donegl 88 A2
An Clochán Liath
  Donegl 88 A2
An Coireán Kerry 82 B3
An Daingean Kerry 82 B2
An Fhairche Galway 86 C3

Annalong Down 89 E4
Annestown Watfd 84 C4
An Rinn Watfd 83 F3
An Spidéal Galway 86 C3
Antrim Antrim 89 D2
Ardagh Limrck 83 D2
Ardara Donegl 88 A2
Ardee Louth 89 D4
Ardfert Kerry 82 C2
Ardfinnan Tippry 84 C4
Ardglass Down 89 E3
Ardgroom Cork 82 B3
Ardmore Watfd 83 E3
Arklow Wicklw 85 E3
Arless Laois 85 D3
Armagh Armagh 89 D3
Armoy Antrim 89 D1
Arthurstown Wexfd 85 D4
Arvagh Cavan 88 B4
Ashbourne Meath 85 E1

Ashford Wicklw 85 E2
Askeaton Limrck 83 D1
Athboy Meath 85 D1
Athea Limrck 82 C2
Athenry Galway 87 D3
Athleague Roscom 87 D3
Athlone Wmeath 84 C1
Athy Kildre 85 D2
Augher Tyrone 88 C3
Aughnacloy Tyrone 88 C3
Aughrim Wicklw 85 E3
Avoca Wicklw 85 E3

B

Bagenalstown Carlow 85 D3
Baile Mhic Íre Cork 82 C3
Bailieborough Cavan 88 C4
Balbriggan Dublin 85 E1
Balla Mayo 86 C2

Ballaghaderreen
  Roscom 87 D2
Ballina Mayo 86 C2
Ballina Tippry 83 D1
Ballinagh Cavan 88 C4
Ballinakill Laois 84 C3
Ballinalee Longfd 88 B4
Ballinamallard Ferman 88 B3
Ballinamore Leitrm 88 B4
Ballinascarty Cork 83 D3
Ballinasloe Galway 87 D3
Ballindine Mayo 86 C3
Ballineen Cork 83 D3
Ballingarry Limrck 83 D2
Ballingarry Tippry 84 C3
Ballingeary Cork 82 C3
Ballinhassig Cork 83 D3
Ballinlough Roscom 87 D2
Ballinrobe Mayo 86 C3

Ballinspittle Cork 83 D3
Ballintober Roscom 87 D2
Ballintra Donegl 88 B3
Ballivor Meath 85 D1
Ballon Carlow 85 D3
Ballybaun Galway 87 D3
Ballybay Monhan 88 C4
Ballybofey Donegl 88 B2
Ballybunion Kerry 82 C2
Ballycanew Wexfd 85 E3
Ballycarry Antrim 89 E2
Ballycastle Antrim 89 D1
Ballycastle Mayo 86 C1
Ballyclare Antrim 89 E2
Ballycolla Laois 84 C3
Ballyconneely Galway 86 B3
Ballyconnell Cavan 88 B4
Ballycotton Cork 83 E3
Ballycumber Offaly 84 C2
Ballydehob Cork 82 C4
Ballydesmond Cork 82 C2
Ballyduff Kerry 82 C2
Ballyduff Watfd 84 B4
Ballyfarnan Roscom 87 D2
Ballygalley Antrim 89 E2
Ballygar Galway 87 D3
Ballygawley Sligo 87 D1
Ballygawley Tyrone 88 C3
Ballygowan Down 89 E3
Ballyhack Wexfd 85 D4
Ballyhaise Cavan 88 C4
Ballyhale Kilken 85 D3
Ballyhaunis Mayo 87 D2
Ballyhean Mayo 86 C2
Ballyheige Kerry 82 B2
Ballyjamesduff Cavan 88 C4
Ballykeeran Wmeath 84 C1
Ballylanders Limrck 83 E2
Ballylickey Cork 82 C3
Ballyliffin Donegl............88 C1
Ballylongford Kerry 82 C2
Ballylooby Tippry 84 B4
Ballylynan Laois..............85 D2
Ballymacarbry Watfd 84 C4
Ballymahon Longfd 84 C1
Ballymakeery Cork 82 C3
Ballymena Antrim 89 D2
Ballymoe Galway 87 D3
Ballymoney Antrim..........89 D2
Ballymore Wmeath 84 C1
Ballymore Eustace
 Kildre 85 D2
Ballymote Sligo 87 D2
Ballynahinch Down 89 E3
Ballynure Antrim.............89 E2
Ballyporeen Tippry..........84 B4
Ballyragget Kilken 84 C3
Ballyroan Laois 84 C2
Ballyronan Lderry 89 D2
Ballysadare Sligo............87 D1
Ballyshannon Donegl......87 D1
Ballyvaughan Clare 86 C4
Ballywalter Down 89 E3
Balrothery Dublin 85 E1
Baltimore Cork 82 C4
Baltinglass Wicklw 85 D2
Banagher Offaly 84 B2
Banbridge Down 89 D3
Bandon Cork 83 D3
Bangor Down..................89 E2
Bangor Erris Mayo 86 B2
Bansha Tippry 84 B3
Banteer Cork 83 D2
Bantry Cork 82 C3
Barna Galway..................86 C3

Béal an Mhuirhead
 Mayo...........................86 B1
Béal Átha an
 Ghaorthaidh Cork......82 C3
Bearna Galway 86 C3
Beaufort Kerry................82 C3
Belcoo Ferman 87 E1
Belfast Belfst 89 E3
Belgooly Cork 83 D3
Bellaghy Lderry 89 D2
Belleek Ferman...............87 D1
Belmullet Mayo 86 B1
Belturbet Cavan 88 C4
Belview Port Kilken.........85 D4
Benburb Tyrone..............89 D3
Bennettsbridge Kilken 85 D3
Beragh Tyrone 88 C3
Bettystown Meath...........85 E1
Birr Offaly 84 C2
Blacklion Cavan 87 E1
Blackrock Dublin 85 E2
Blackwater Wexfd 85 E3
Blarney Cork 83 D3
Blessington Wicklw 85 D2
Boherbue Cork 83 D2
Borris Carlow..................85 D3
Borris-in-Ossory Laois 84 C2
Borrisokane Tippry 87 D4
Borrisoleigh Tippry 84 C3
Boyle Roscom 87 D2
Bracknagh Offaly 85 D2
Bray Wicklw 85 E2
Bridgetown Wexfd 85 D4
Brittas Dublin 85 E2
Broadford Clare 83 D1
Broadford Limrck 83 D2
Broughshane Antrim........89 D2
Bruff Limrck 83 D2
Bruree Limrck 83 D2
Bunbeg Donegl 88 B2
Bunclody Wexfd 85 D3
Buncrana Donegl 88 C1
Bundoran Donegl 87 D1
Bunmahon Watfd 84 C4
Bun na hAbhna Mayo......86 B1
Bunnahowen Mayo 86 B1
Bunnyconnellan Mayo.....86 C2
Bunratty Clare 83 D1
Burnfort Cork 83 D3
Bushmills Antrim.............89 D1
Buttevant Cork 83 D2

C

Cadamstown Offaly.........84 C2
Caherconlish Limrck 83 D1
Caherdaniel Kerry 82 B3
Cahersiveen Kerry 82 B3
Cahir Tippry 84 C4
Caledon Tyrone 88 C3
Callan Kilken 84 C3
Caltra Galway 87 D3
Camp Kerry 82 B2
Campile Wexfd 85 D4
Cappagh White Tippry.....84 B3
Cappamore Limrck...........83 E1
Cappoquin Watfd 84 C4
Carlanstown Meath.........85 D1
Carlingford Louth 89 D4
Carlow Carlow.................85 D3
Carna Galway 86 B3
Carndonagh Donegl 88 C1
Carnew Wicklw 85 E3
Carnlough Antrim 89 E2
Carracastle Mayo............87 D2

Carraig Airt Donegl 88 B1
Carrick Donegl 88 A2
Carrickart Donegl............88 B1
Carrickfergus Antrim 89 E2
Carrickmacross
 Monhan 89 D4
Carrickmore or
 Termon Rock
 Tyrone 88 C3
Carrick-on-Shannon
 Leitrm 87 D2
Carrick-on-Suir Tippry.....84 C4
Carrigahorig Tippry..........87 D4
Carrigaline Cork 83 D3
Carrigallen Leitrm 88 B4
Carriganimmy Cork 83 D3
Carrigans Donegl 88 C2
Carrigtohill Cork 83 E3
Carryduff Down 89 E3
Cashel Galway.................86 B3
Cashel Tippry 84 C3
Castlebar Mayo 86 C2
Castlebellingham
 Louth 89 D4
Castleblayney
 Monhan 89 D4
Castlebridge Wexfd 85 E4
Castlecomer Laois 85 D3
Castleconnell Limrck 83 D1
Castlederg Tyrone 88 B2
Castledermot Kildre........83 D3
Castlegregory Kerry 82 B2
Castleisland Kerry 82 C2
Castlemaine Kerry...........82 C2
Castlemartyr Cork 83 E3
Castleplunket Roscom.....87 D2
Castlepollard Wmeath.....84 C1
Castlerea Roscom 87 D2
Castlerock Lderry 88 C1
Castleshane Monhan 88 C3
Castletown Laois 84 C2
Castletownbere Cork.......82 B3
Castletownroche
 Cork 83 D2
Castletownshend
 Cork 82 C4
Castlewellan Down 89 E3
Cathair Dónall Kerry 82 B3
Causeway Kerry 82 C2
Cavan Cavan...................88 C4
Celbridge Kildre..............85 D2
Charlestown Mayo...........86 C2
Charleville Cork 83 D2
Cheekpoint Watfd 85 D4
Cill Charthaigh
 Donegl 88 A2
Cill Chiaráin Galway 86 B3
Clady Tyrone 88 C2
Clane Kildre 85 D2
Clara Offaly 84 C2
Clarecastle Clare 83 D1
Claremorris Mayo............86 C2
Clarinbridge Galway 86 C3
Clashmore Watfd 83 E3
Claudy Lderry 88 C2
Clifden Galway 86 B3
Cliffony Sligo 87 D1
Clogh Kilken...................85 D3
Cloghan Offaly 84 C2
Clogheen Tippry 84 B4
Clogher Tyrone 88 C3
Clohamon Wexfd 85 D3
Clonakilty Cork 83 D4
Clonard Meath 85 D1
Clonaslee Laois 84 C2

Clonbulloge Offaly 85 D2
Clonbur Galway 86 C3
Clondalkin Dublin 85 E2
Clones Monhan 88 C3
Clonlara Clare 83 D1
Clonmany Donegl 88 C1
Clonmel Tippry 84 C4
Clonmellon Wmeath........85 D1
Clonmore Tippry 84 C3
Clonony Offaly 84 C2
Clonoulty Tippry 84 B3
Clonroche Wexfd 85 D3
Clontibret Monhan..........88 C3
Cloondara Longfd 84 C1
Clough Down 89 E3
Cloughjordan Tippry........87 D4
Cloyne Cork 83 E3
Coagh Tyrone 89 D2
Coalisland Tyrone 89 D3
Cobh Cork.......................83 E3
Coleraine Lderry 89 D1
Collinstown Wmeath 85 D1
Collon Louth...................89 D4
Collooney Sligo 87 D1
Comber Down 89 E3
Cong Mayo 86 C3
Conna Cork 83 E3
Cookstown Tyrone...........89 D2
Coole Wmeath 84 C1
Cooraclare Clare..............82 C1
Cootehill Cavan...............88 C4
Cork Cork........................83 D3
Cornamona Galway 86 C3
Corr na Móna Galway......86 C3
Corrofin Clare 86 C4
Courtmacsherry
 Cork 83 D4
Courtown Wexfd..............85 E3
Craigavon Armagh..........89 D3
Craughwell Galway..........87 D3
Crawfordsburn Down.......89 E2
Creegs Galway.................87 D3
Creeslough Donegl..........88 B1
Croagh Limrck.................83 D2
Croithli Donegl................88 B2
Crolly Donegl..................88 B2
Crookedwood
 Wmeath.......................84 C1
Crookhaven Cork.............82 C4
Crookstown Cork 83 D3
Croom Limrck..................83 D2
Crossakeel Meath............85 D1
Cross Barry Cork 83 D3
Crosshaven Cork.............83 E3
Crossmaglen Armagh.......89 D4
Crossmolina Mayo 86 C2
Crumlin Antrim 89 D2
Crusheen Clare 86 C4
Culdaff Donegl................88 C1
Cullybackey Antrim 89 D2
Curracloe Wexfd..............85 E4
Curraghboy Roscom 87 D3
Curry Sligo......................87 D2
Cushendall Antrim...........89 D2
Cushendun Antrim...........89 D1

D

Daingean Offaly...............84 C2
Delgany Wicklw 85 E2
Delvin Wmeath 85 D1
Derry Lderry 88 C2
Derrygonnelly Ferman.....87 E1
Derrylin Ferman 88 B3
Dervock Antrim................89 D1